1684

THE DISCERNMENT OF VOCATIONS

THE DISCERNMENT
OF VOCATIONS

R. HOSTIE, S.J.

Translated by Michael Barry

SHEED & WARD—NEW YORK

This book was first published in 1962 by Desclée de Brouwer et Cie, under the title *Le discernment des vocations*.

© translation, 1963, Geoffrey Chapman Ltd.

Library of Congress Catalogue Card Number: 63-10493

Nihil obstat   Daniel Duivesteijn, S.T.D. *Censor deputatus.*
Imprimatur   E. Morrogh Bernard, *Vic. Gen.*
Westmonasterii,   die 15a Novembris, 1962

The Nihil obstat *and* Imprimatur *are a declaration that a book or pamphlet is considered to be free from doctrinal or moral error. It is not implied that those who have granted the* Nihil obstat *and* Imprimatur *agree with the contents, opinions, or statements expressed.*

MADE AND PRINTED IN GREAT BRITAIN

CONTENTS

IV. THE DISCERNMENT OF INTERNAL VOCATION

V. HOW DECISIONS ARE MADE KNOWN

VI. DISCERNING VOCATIONS IN PRACTICE

CONCLUSION

THE DISCERNMENT OF VOCATIONS AS A WORK OF COLLABORATION

PREFACE

THIS work of Reverend Father Raymond Hostie, which it is our pleasure to present to the reader, answers a real need.

The progress of medical and psychological science has not only drawn attention to the numerous and more or less unconscious bio-psychical implications in the choice of a vocation, but it has also made it possible to gain more accurate knowledge about the various essential aspects of a person's growth to maturity, a condition which is more than ever necessary for the candidate to the priesthood or religious life. At the same time the supreme authority of the Church has repeatedly and insistently demanded of the superiors responsible that they should pay the greatest heed to the psychological aspects of the question when recognizing vocations and preparing candidates. Indeed, because of present-day sociological conditions, it is more than ever important for the liberty and right intention of candidates to the priesthood or religious life to be examined carefully and skilfully.

Under these conditions a study of the different aspects of the discernment of vocations became both necessary and possible. The value of this introduction to the problems of discerning vocations is vouched for by the author, who has been trained in theology and psychology and whose experience in helping and advising a great number of superiors, spiritual directors and candidates has brought him real competence in the field. The viewpoints of theological tradition, as well as the data of modern science, are given their rightful place here. We sincerely hope that this preliminary study may be followed by other works in which the various aspects are investigated thoroughly on the theoretical as well as the practical level.

P. ANCIAUX,
Président Du Grand Séminaire,
Malines

INTRODUCTION

The discernment of vocations has been a practical issue ever since the Church came into being. It was even, so the Acts of the Apostles tells us, the first task the Apostolic College took upon itself after the Ascension.

Bearing in mind Christ's words: 'It was not you that chose me, it was I that chose you' (John, 15:16), the apostles were concerned, at that very first election from among the members of the Church, to make sure that the man replacing Judas should be the Lord's chosen one. When they saw that two candidates were fully qualified, they turned to prayer: 'Lord, who knowest the hearts of all men, show us which of these two thou hast chosen to take his place in this work of apostleship, from which Judas has fallen away' (Acts, 1: 24-5). And they drew lots in order that God might pronounce.

Admittedly the procedure to which the apostles had recourse has been replaced by less charismatic methods; yet it shows that in their eyes any vocation supposes, over and above the required aptitudes, a personal call from God. This call must be recognized objectively, because it stems from God alone.

The author of the Epistle to the Hebrews also stipulates the strictly divine character of the call to the priesthood, emphasizing that the priesthood of Christ himself is no exception: 'Nobody can take on himself such a privilege as this. So it is with Christ. He did not raise himself to the dignity of the high priesthood; it was God that raised him to it, when he said, 'Thou art my Son, I have begotten thee this day' (Heb., 5: 4-5).

The discernment of vocations is not simply a venerable tradition. Now, more than ever, it is a central preoccupation of the Church Numerous publications in spiritual theology on the one hand, and the enormous progress in medical and psychological science on the other, have helped to effect a more systematic approach to many points; and the Church authorities encourage efforts to foster a greater understanding of the complicated problems which recent discoveries have laid bare.★ Hence the discernment of vocations is an important contemporary issue and is not without its difficulties.

I would probably not have ventured to write this book had cir-

★ Of particular importance among the official documents are the following texts, all issued by Sovereign Pontiffs or Roman Congregations. The numbers in brackets refer to the notes in which they feature. The reader can use them as a guide to the contents of the documents.

a) Encyclical *Ad Catholici Sacerdotii* of Pius XI (20th Dec., 1935). A.A.S. (*Acta Apostolicae Sedis*), XXVIII, 1936, pp. 5-53.

(Cf. notes, pp. 87, 105, 112)

b) Apostolic Exhortation *Menti Nostrae* of Pius XII (23rd Sep., 1950). A.A.S., XLII, 1950, pp. 657-702.   (Cf. note, p. 121)

c) Encyclical *Sacra Virginitas* of Pius XII (25th Mar., 1954). A.A.S., XLVI, 1954, pp. 161-91.

d) Instruction *Quam Ingens* of the Sacred Congregation for the Sacra ments (27th Dec., 1930). A.A.S. XXIII, 1931, pp. 120-9. (Cf. note, p.87)

e) Instruction *Quantum Religiones* of the S. Congregation of Religious (1st Dec., 1931). A.A.S., XXIV, 1932, pp. 74-81.

f) Instruction *Magna Equidem* of the S. Congregation for the Sacra ments (27th Dec., 1955). Reservata   (Cf. notes, p. 87, 105, 112)

g) Apostolic Constitution *Sedes Sapientiae* (31st May, 1956). A.A.S. XLVIII, 1956, pp. 354-65.   (Cf. note p. 21)

h) *Statuta Generalia* (appendix to the previous document). Published separately by the S. Congregation of Religious, Rome, 1957, 98 pp.

i) Letter of the S. Congregation of Seminaries to the Hierarchy on the selection and training of candidates to the priesthood (27th Sep., 1960). English translation used here is based on the French in *L'ami du Clergé*, LXX, 17th Nov., 1960, col. 676-84.   (Cf. notes p. 112, 133) cumstances not set me in the thick of the main present-day trends. My formation has benefited from practical and theoretical experience in the fields both of spirituality and of psychology. For several years I have been in charge both of courses in pastoral psychology, intended, for the most part, for young priests starting out on their first ministry; and of study sessions or case-work held with superiors, novice-masters and spiritual directors. At the same time I was invited to help seminarists and religious during their years of formation, as well as priests and religious who had already had their training. Most of this work was with people who were a prey to uncertainty and doubt or who were passing through the trial of some spiritual distress. The help I gave led me naturally to exchanges of opinion with superiors and spiritual directors as well as with medical specialists, whenever the nature of the problems made this necessary or where the subjects asked for it. This gradually led me to take on the rôle of counsellor in certain psycho-religious problems.

From the outset such collaboration went very smoothly—superiors, spiritual directors and specialists showed the widest understanding. But, at the same time, it became evident that the principles were often imperfectly understood and the practical applications often questionable to a degree. This is not to be wondered at. Recent works on vocations are certainly numerous in the field of spiritual and moral theology, but nearly all are speculative. It need hardly be said that this does not detract from their value, but it does mean that little recognition is given to their practical application in the discernment of vocations. Studies of the subject from the medical and psychological angle are fairly rare, at least in dealing with the problem as a whole. There have been valuable articles published in various journals in recent years, but these are confined to particular questions.*

★ Among the books, which are few, published on the medical aspects of discerning vocations, two will be mentioned here. They are among

Circumstances obliged me to study from close quarters the present practice of the Church, to reflect on the whole complex of problems involved, to make allowances for both spiritual and psychological factors and to systematize in a coherent structure the data furnished by experience. The result was this preliminary synthesis which takes its inspiration as closely as possible from the living practice of the Church. The best part of this work is due to all those who have honoured me with their trust: the five hundred or so seminarists, religious, nuns and priests who in long conversations have spoken to me so frankly; almost as many superiors, directors and priests, with widely differing functions, who have submitted the subtle problems and complex situations they have come across in their work and who have shown their agreement or sent their observations about the solutions put forward or the advice given; and lastly the specialists who so kindly collaborated and willingly took part in discussions and exchanges

---

the most recently published, although they date from 1943 and 1947. The first is a doctorate thesis submitted to the medical faculty at Lyons by J. Géraud, priest of Saint-Sulpice, and entitled: *Contre-indications médicales à l'orientation vers le clergé* (Lyons, Vitte, 1947, 239 pp). The second is less technical. Edited by two doctors of long experience, R. Biot and P. Galimard, it is, despite its title (*Guide Médical des vocations sacerdotales et religieuses*: Paris, Spes, 1952, 367 pp.), addressed to all priests and in particular to superiors.

Certain psychological aspects have been studied by A. Benkö and J. Nuttin. *Examen de la personnalité chez les candidats à la prêtrise* (Louvain, Publications Universitaires, 1956, 139 pp). There is a good bibliography (pp. 110-116). Very good articles have been published particularly in the reviews *Supplément de la Vie Spirituelle* and *Nouvelle Revue Théologique*, and some studies of greater scope in the collections *Etudes Carmélitaines* and *Problèmes de la Religieuse d'Aujourd'hui* (Paris, Cerf, out of print). A bibliography, not exhaustive but carefully drawn up, of these publications is given in the *Supplément de la Vie Spirituelle*, no. 49, 1959, pp. 177-82.

In 1959, J. Géraud published a 'memento' entitled: *Itinéraire médico-psychologique de la vocation* (Le Puy, Mappus, 94 pp).

of opinion. Without them this work could not have been brought to any satisfactory conclusion.

But this essay in synthesis has its limits. It is centred entirely round a single theme, the discernment of vocations. It touches lightly on various problems and passes on, without going into detail. For this reason it calls for complementary works which deal more thoroughly with pastoral care (its basic laws and precise techniques), individual problems (such as those to do with faith or sexual difficulties) and psychic disturbances (neuroses and psychoses). These subjects seemed too important and extensive to be presented as an appendix to this book, and they deserve a more thorough treatment in volumes which I hope to publish later. On the other hand it seemed that the present subject formed a sufficiently coherent whole. Its aim, in effect, is simply to enlighten priests, directors, and religious superiors—and perhaps even those specialists who are interested—about what can be done in the sphere of everyday practice.

Starting from the solid foundations of the Church's doctrine and practice, I have attempted to make clear what those responsible for discerning vocations both can and must do, what specific competence they must have, and what limits they may not exceed without risk of causing harm. They can then go ahead with their task with greater assurance. They will have a clear idea of what lies within their own competence and will understand when and why they may have to call in the complementary skills of others.

With this end in view the book has been planned as follows. The first chapter clarifies a few general definitions: it is very short and could hardly be otherwise. Any exposition, however incomplete, of the spiritual theology of vocation would have needed to be developed at length and would have exceeded the framework of this volume: so I have intentionally limited myself to bare essentials. The reader is asked to remember this in view of the brevity of this chapter. The second chapter examines those who are entrusted with the discernment of vocations and points out the responsibility and scope proper to each. The third and fourth chapters can then establish how discernment works in the two fields of external and internal vocation. And finally the fifth chapter studies how discernment is communicated to the parties concerned. The whole of this central section of the book is concerned with the examination of the broad framework of discernment. Thus, from the outset particular problems have only been dealt with within the living and actual continuity of any and every vocation. Only in the sixth chapter do we come to the practical application of these general rules to the particular situations of the candidates, according to their age. This arrangement of the subject matter may seem confusing at first sight. Certainly the procedure is not chronological, but it has the advantage of avoiding repetition, and also it allows the actual steps in discernment to be fitted into the process of growth towards the full flowering of vocation.

The reader is requested to bear three points in mind while reading this book.

In order not to load the text with fastidious distinctions, frequent use has been made of 'common denominators'. These permit several categories of people to be put under one heading. The words 'superiors' and 'candidates' indicate superiors and candidates of the secular and religious clergy as well as those of a religious congregation. By candidates are understood young men or women offering themselves for admission to a seminary or noviciate as well as those in their period of formation. Wherever these terms are used in a more restricted sense the exact differences are indicated.

For the same reason no distinction is made between vocations to the religious life and the secular or religious priesthood unless such a distinction is definitely required. This procedure is not admissible when a study is being made of the different forms of vocation, but it is valid when discernment is being spoken of. In this case, indeed, the attempt is made to bring out the criteria by which the authenticity of a divine call in general and the particular direction taken in individual vocations may be recognized.

This book will only be of use if the principles laid down and the procedures described are judiciously applied by competent persons. To put it into the hands of persons in distress or candidates who are hesitant or uncertain will not solve any problems and may even aggravate the trouble.

The writer wishes to give his sincere thanks to his colleagues and fellow-religious who have so kindly read these pages before publication and offered their criticisms, which have greatly contributed to the arrangement of the work and the restatement of delicate problems which abound in such a subject.

CHAPTER I

VOCATIONS

EVERYDAY language contains many overtones and nuances. This is what gives it such wealth, but this very wealth can stand in the way of clarity, giving rise to misunderstandings when exact meanings are lost in a captivating brilliance. Anyone who talks about vocations is exposed to this danger.

1. VOCATIONS IN SPIRITUAL THEOLOGY

The word 'vocation' is to be found over and over again in spiritual writing, and in ordinary life both directors and directed, superiors and subjects, use it ceaselessly: 'Everyone thought she had a vocation; she was an exemplary novice'; 'Is that sort of work in keeping with our vocation?'; 'He had everything which goes to make a good priest, but he hadn't got a vocation!'. The same word every time, but the realities covered by it differ greatly. Sometimes exterior behaviour is meant, sometimes the personal assumption of a certain type of life, sometimes a strictly interior reality.

And so the first thing to be done is to define very clearly what is meant by vocation. A limitation must be set to its terms and characteristics and this can be done by reference to the doctrines commonly held by theologians and spiritual writers. It is true that they often seem to be in disagreement. The Church's teaching authority has made scarcely any definitive pronouncements on these matters and theologians have been able to give free rein to their personal reflections. Upon closer study, however, there turns out to be a very real agreement on principles. Our sole concern here is with this agreement on principles, and no discussion will be undertaken of individual positions and the controversies between various schools. However desirable and useful such a discussion may be, it forms no part of the work immediately in hand.

Man's nature is what it is by the creative summons of God. He is raised to the supernatural life through sanctifying grace by a personal acceptance of the redemptive gesture of this same God. Man can then perform supernatural acts whose purpose is to let him share in the divine life. However, in more difficult or exceptional circumstances God grants special supernatural aid which is attributed by appropriation to the Holy Spirit. This is commonly known as an 'inspiration'. This help, granted to man for some particular requirement, takes the form of internal graces or actual graces in the proper sense, as opposed to external graces, called actual graces by analogy. These external graces are all the divine aids in the order of natural causes: character, talents, influences of environment, education, example, preaching, etc.

It should further be noted that any internal grace is both a light which helps us recognize the will of God (even in natural causes) and a force which leads us on to accomplish what we have perceived. An internal grace is thus a supernatural dynamism which enlightens us as to the end to which it is leading us. This light and force must not be conceived as two different entities, not even complementary ones. Grace invests and moulds the whole being and so has its repercussions in the faculties. In moving the will it directs the understanding, and in enlightening the understanding it attracts the will.

Vocation, in so far as it is a divine call, is generally conceived as an internal grace. This gives a greater understanding of its characteristics: it is purely gratuitous, absolutely free and strictly supernatural.

Vocation is *gratuitous:* it hardly needs saying that it is by no means a natural right of human nature. And what is more, it is by no means necessary for full participation in the supernatural life, once this has been conferred on man. Certainly community life in accordance with the counsels is a privileged way of participating in the fullness of God, and sacramental participation in the priesthood of Christ prints an indelible mark on the priest's being; but neither this way of life nor this sacerdotal character is required in order to come to the fullness of faith in this world or to that of the beatific vision in the next.

Vocation is *free:* it summons, not to the fundamental participation in the divine life but to a particular mode of more immediate and exclusive participation. To refuse it, even deliberately and with full knowledge, does not imply any fundamental rejection of the Lord or any complete turning back to creatures. This is why certain moralists say that failure to heed a vocation does not constitute a sin. It should be stressed, however, that such a refusal does at least constitute the missing of an important opportunity. A morality which is mainly pre-occupied with rights and duties has a tendency to fit everything into the categories of sin and not sin, taking hardly any account of charity and fidelity. In the human order, the refusal of a proffered friendship does not constitute an injustice. But this does not mean that such a refusal, if conscious and deliberate, is any the less inhuman: it spoils and degrades a man, even though it does not destroy him in his being, since no right has been infringed. With even more reason will the rejection of a friendship which is firm and flourishing have profound repercussions. The friend who has been rejected feels himself more hurt, stricken and impoverished by this act than he would from some flagrant injustice. To say that the refusal of a vocation does not constitute a sin does not mean we are minimizing its importance,

its value and religious significance, but rather that we place a vocation at the heart of the supernatural order, in the category of
loyalty, which is characterized by kindness, spontaneity and consideration, and not by peremptory commands, rights and duties.

Vocation is *strictly supernatural:* in itself it has nothing in
common with the miraculous and even less with the marvellous.
A vocation may be manifested in a more or less miraculous way
(as in the frequently cited case of St Paul, where it was accompanied by voices and visions), but this is purely adventitious. The
increasingly fine distinction drawn nowadays between mystical
experiences and paramystical phenomena throws light on this
point. The former all lead to a more or less immediate and ineffable
participation in the divine life through an intensification of the
theological virtues of faith, hope and charity; while the latter
embrace all the more or less sensible manifestations either perceived by the subject (visions, voices, sensible contacts of the soul,
etc.), or objectively verifiable by witnesses (ecstasies, stigmatiza-
tion, levitation etc.).

Since vocation as an internal grace has nothing to do with the
miraculous, it is not bound up with sensibility either. Any sensible
overflowing not of a paranormal character (attractions, desires,
delights, consolations, etc.) is accidental, though this need not
mean inauthentic or illusory. But such attractions or desires may
arise from purely human causes, without there being any internal
grace at work in the soul. In this case, illusion lies in treating them
as signs of vocation. Moreover, this internal grace can be very active
while the sensibility either remains listless and sluggish or rises in
rebellion.

2. VOCATION: EXTERNAL AND INTERNAL, DIVINE AND ECCLESIASTICAL

Hitherto, we have attempted to determine what internal vocation consists of by contrasting it with external graces; but it must not be forgotten that internal and external graces come together in certain favoured people, since they proceed from the one Lord who dispenses them both. By asking ourselves what activity is proper to the internal grace of vocation it is possible for us to draw disparate elements into one coherent whole.

Now, God gives rise to a vocation inasmuch as he is the Sanctifier. He is also the Creator, who has given rise not only to this person whom he is calling but also to the whole environment through which the call is made. The Lord's fidelity lies in continuity and cohesion; he has prepared, disposed and endowed the one whom he is calling, with a view to this call. It would be unthinkable for God to call anyone without granting him, at least germinally, the required aptitudes. But these aptitudes (which will be considered in more detail later) do not belong exclusively to those who have the priestly or religious vocation. So God has to intervene to make the individual realize the significance of these external graces for him. Internal grace gradually makes him aware that everything in his life combines to direct him towards the priesthood or religious life, and more and more urgently invites him to take freely upon himself the call which is becoming ever clearer.

And so it is not surprising that the Church, in its most authoritative documents, takes the term 'divine vocation' to mean the sum total of these external and internal graces. The Church distinguishes it from 'ecclesiastical vocation', which is constituted by the call of the residing bishop or a major superior admitting to perpetual profession.★ With the Church's mandate they ratify in

---

★ The distinction between divine and ecclesiastical vocation as well as their complementary character is clearly set out by the Apostolic Constitution *Sedes Sapientiae* (¶13-17). It is explicitly said here that this distinction applies equally to the religious state and to vocations to the priesthood. Since this is the most recent official document on the subject, it has been thought advisable to keep to its terminology and its definitions.

the name of God what God has given rise to in the soul. Until this definitive ratification has taken place no one can say for certain that he has been called. On the other hand, in so far as it is a ratification, the ecclesiastical vocation can do nothing more than recognize the divine vocation. And where the divine vocation is lacking —even if, in all good faith, this is not realized—the ecclesiastical vocation can never make up for it nor create it out of nothing.

For these reasons, both the subjects who ask 'Have I a vocation?' and the bishops or major superiors who wonder 'Can I be sure whether he has a vocation?' find themselves up against the same problem: How is the divine vocation to be discerned?

Before proceeding to the next chapter, we must go over a few brief definitions. Vocation is basically an internal grace by which God unites himself to the man whom he consecrates to himself and calls either to the duties of a priest or to the life of the evangelical counsels. This grace, like some supernatural dynamism, makes the subject aware that everything in his life combines to lead him to take upon himself freely, and with the Church's approbation, a form of life recognized (or to be recognized) by the Church. Consequently four types of vocation can be distinguished: internal, external, divine and ecclesiastical. The first applies to the internal grace, the second to the sum total of aptitudes or external graces, the third embraces the first two, and the fourth refers to the call from the superiors authorized by the Church. When the ecclesiastical vocation authentically includes all the foregoing elements, then it is morally certain that a vocation exists.

The reader, then, should notice that this terminology differs from the one used by St Thomas Aquinas. St Thomas also talks of internal and external vocation, but by the former he means divine vocation and by the latter ecclesiastical vocation.

When reference is made in this book to the bishop responsible for discerning vocations, this obviously means the bishop who is the Ordinary of the diocese.

CHAPTER II

THOSE RESPONSIBLE FOR DISCERNMENT

THE discernment of vocations is essentially concerned with divine vocation. Its aim is with the aid of valid criteria to recognize the presence of the necessary external and internal graces in a subject. But before even examining more closely the way to go about this, it is necessary to know who is responsible for the task of discernment. At first sight the answer is very simple. Since God himself officially delegates the representatives recognized by the Church, they alone are the ones to occupy themselves with this delicate task. It is a good thing to emphasize this right and duty of bishops and major superiors very vigorously, and this point will certainly be returned to.

1. THE HIERARCHY OF THOSE RESPONSIBLE FOR DISCERNMENT

On reflection, however, it appears that the answer is not as simple as some people like to think. Everyday practice in the selection and admission of candidates, and the formation and preparation of seminarists and young religious shows very clearly that bishops and major superiors are obliged to turn to many collaborators for assistance.

In many religious congregations the constitutions or customs approved by the Church even provide that not only official collaborators or a restricted and duly selected council, but also all members of the community, should be entitled to give their opinion about admission to profession.

Cases also arise, and they are not infrequent, where judgment on a particular point makes the help of a specialist necessary. Persistent doubts about a state of physical or mental health, and the more or less suspect origins of certain religious or paramystical phenomena, all demand the intervention of a qualified doctor or theologian. In this way there is established a whole hierarchy of permanent or occasional collaborators whose help is necessary. All of them, however, receive their respective tasks directly from the superiors and are subordinate to them in carrying them out.

This is not all. The subject who offers himself to a superior has himself taken the first step. He undertakes such a step only in the conviction that it is good and justified, while realizing that it depends on later ratification. Even before offering himself to the superior or being known by him he has had to decide for himself whether there was any reason to think he had a vocation.

With very few exceptions, he will not have made the decision without taking advice. This is simply plain sense. He will have turned to a priest whom he felt he could trust or who was recommended to him. This priest will have guided and directed him, and explained what a vocation to the priestly or religious life is. He will have helped him to see more clearly the character of the particular call which was made to him and have endeavoured to weigh up the authenticity of his desire. All this will finally have culminated in a step taken in a particular direction and offering serious guarantees. The fact that the internal vocation is manifested in the soul while remaining generally confused as to its origins requires the help of a priest, be he a permanent director or an occasional adviser. Every priest, in fact, receives a general mandate from the Church through the jurisdiction which is conferred on him.

This priest, however, gives his help without having any clearly defined mandate or any direct contact with the superior, and this only makes the task more delicate. He is frequently the first adviser to whom the candidate opens himself: his attitude, principles and advice will have far-reaching effects. And so he must realize that all his help is conditioned, as it must always be, by the ultimate ratification of the competent superior.

Both directors and directed are sometimes ill-informed about this. Directors in their zeal, candidates in their enthusiasm, forget that in any vocation it is a question of seeking the will of God, not of acquiescing in any human will. However lofty the aim proposed, whatever the intrinsic value of the gift envisaged, there is no justification for a step which is not furthered by a divine vocation, corroborated by the guardians of the priestly or religious life.

It is by no means rare to come across embittered and unhappy people, convinced that the refusal given them by competent superiors is in flagrant contradiction with the call of God, which they once thought, and still do think, to be addressed to them. Certain directors sometimes let themselves be led on to foster or even to stir up such feelings. It need hardly be said that people given such direction bear throughout their lives the bitterness of having been turned down. They think themselves failures, and before long they are past recovery.

Occasionally, such a misunderstanding of the superior's rôle has an even more tragic sequel. By insistence and much manoeuvring —for evidently the end justifies the means in cases like this—some candidates do manage to get themselves accepted for permanent commitment. It is hardly surprising that they become a burden as much to their community as to their own selves for the rest of their lives.

For this reason not only superiors and their immediate collaborators but also all priests must be duly experienced in matters concerning discernment, for sooner or later they will be approached by candidates. It would be extremely regrettable if genuine candidates were turned away from their vocation by clumsy handling or an erroneous judgment. And it would be no less harmful should they follow their vocation guided by misunderstood principles or fallacious reasoning.

Everything that has been said in the last few paragraphs applies naturally to the major superiors of congregations of brothers and nuns as well as to those who collaborate with them. They also have an official mandate from the Church and must decide in the last resort whether or not to take on the candidates who offer themselves. A clear and accurate idea of how to discern vocations should indeed be expected from every religious, particularly those who are engaged in the active life. Their teaching or social activities regularly put them in contact with young people.

Just as the priest who gives direction or advice must consider himself subordinate to the superior as regards the ultimate discernment, so the religious, having no official responsibility, must consider himself or herself subordinate to the priest for the direct and immediate discernment. But to understand the reasons for this subordination they must see it as a part of the question of vocations as a whole, for by so doing their information, advice and encouragement will gain in objectivity and clarity.

After all, it is normal for a young man or young woman to turn for information to a religious whom they know and esteem, from living in daily contact with them. Often they will do this with a sort of bashfulness, approaching the subject indirectly and taking a long time to get to the point. This is one more reason why those called upon should be able to answer clearly and relevantly. There is, of course, no question of true discernment here, not even in a preliminary sense; but such conversations are only really fruitful if the impetus and direction resulting from them are given in good earnest.

2. THE BISHOP OR MAJOR SUPERIOR AND THEIR DELEGATES AND ADVISERS

Permanent admission is and remains reserved to bishops or major superiors. They can delegate collaborators in accordance with established rules or accepted customs.

This delegation may be total. In a large order or an extensive diocese the final discernment is entrusted to the provincial superior or the superior of the seminary, assisted by their advisers. The bishop or major superior bases his judgment on the report which is made to him, sometimes without any personal acquaintance with the candidate. This does not detract from the authenticity of his decision. It is a real and effective delegation, the extent of which is fixed only by the will of the competent superiors themselves or by duly confirmed prescriptions.

In other cases occasional collaborators are called on. They are responsible for giving their decision on some particular point: state of health, psychic balance, so-called extraordinary phenomena, etc., and the judgment asked for is not about the vocation as such. The specialists consulted should always keep this in mind. They are asked to work within more restricted limits. All the same they should not fail to point out the relevance of the matters they have to examine to the vocation as a whole. But the question put to them and the conclusions they come to could never on their own be decisive. It is for the superior to fit their conclusions into the pattern of information he makes use of in arriving at a definitive decision.

Should the specialists not be aware of the limits of their task they run the risk of troubling the minds of those who consult them and bringing about disastrous confusion. A doctor who discovers a latent but serious illness would be going beyond his competence were he to state that there is therefore no vocation, as would also a psychiatrist who brings to light some mental immaturity. In the same way, a theologian who declares that certain paramystical phenomena are repercussions of authentic supernatural graces in the psychological make-up of the subject would be overstepping the mark if he laid down without any more ado that there is therefore a vocation.

All these specialists are called in strictly 'for consultation'. They have received no delegation, which in any case they are generally not in a position to assume. Without detracting at all from the importance of their functions—for the problems submitted to them are delicate and need great skill, and the repercussions of their advice are sometimes very considerable—it is necessary to set the limits very exactly. The superiors too must be aware of these limits and make sure, even before sending a candidate, that the specialist knows what is required of him. If need be, they must very clearly define his mandate for him.

Sometimes, too, a danger exists that superiors may be tempted to lay aside their responsibility and put the decision into the hands of a specialist. This is particularly so when a subject insists on being kept on when they want to send him away or when they fear to bring upon themselves difficulties or reproaches from the family or patrons of candidates judged unsuitable.

In such cases the superior would do well to ask himself whether he has not had recourse to the specialist merely to escape his own responsibilities. If he is not resolved to give his authoritative backing to the specialist's conclusion—either for or against—in the matter under dispute, or alternatively to present the retention or dismissal of the candidate as a personal decision, then he may be sure that he is sliding out of a responsibility which he may not decline without falling short of his duty. What is more, he is making the specialist a sort of puppet whose strings may be manipulated at will, and this often provokes legitimate resentment on the part of the specialist. The subject who is the victim of these manoeuvres instinctively senses the ambiguity of the situation and will often give vent to his dissatisfaction by a determined resentment, which will only make his readaptation all the more difficult later on.

It may seem that we labour the importance and definitive character of the judgment made by the bishop or major superior; but this is not without reason. Occasionally the scope of their judgment is belittled or called into doubt, with allusion to the man or (where suitable collaborators have been used) the men who promulgate it, whereas in fact this judgment receives its whole validity from the due exercise of the official function of the bishop or superior. And so, if the process of discerning a vocation comes finally to refusal or dismissal, the candidate should take this as meaning that there is no reason for him to believe that he is called, at any rate not to that way of life represented by the superior in question: not to that particular order or diocese.

Collaborators in all spheres, and spiritual directors above all, would do well to proclaim their full agreement with this principle, which proceeds from a correct understanding of faith. It goes without saying that before any superior gives his definitive decision, both the candidate and the collaborators can and must make known all the facts at their disposal in order to make things as clear as possible for the superior. But the final decision must be considered, assuming there has been no deception or dishonesty, as an indication of providence. This is not to claim any infallibility for superiors but simply to plead for supernatural prudence on the part of the collaborators as well as of the directors and those they direct.

3. THE CANDIDATES, THEIR ADVISERS AND DIRECTORS

A negative decision should therefore be taken by the candidate as an intimation of God's will; but it is not to be thought that a positive decision absolves the candidate from all personal examination of his vocation.

This is firstly because the superior can only discern the vocation, particularly in so far as it is a question of internal vocation, if the candidate is perfectly open. Even more, though, because vocations always presuppose a completely free acceptance. The candidate's assent must spring from a deep conviction that it is an answer to a call made by God. If he says: 'The bishop is calling me, and so I must give my consent', there is an alienation of freedom at the very root of this commitment which of its very nature is utterly personal. If, however, he says: 'The bishop is calling me, and so I *can* give my consent', he is speaking the truth. But this truth has its conditions: assuming that all the obstacles have been cleared, he must personally be certain that his consent is an answer to which he will conform with his whole being.

In this personal search for his vocation every candidate can receive assistance from the qualified collaborators called in by the superiors. Their respective competence has already been indicated. Their contribution will have mainly to do with external graces since matters of conscience are not generally accessible to them.

The spiritual director or occasional adviser will be the guides suggested for the discernment of internal graces. These priests, thanks to their mission as confessors, are in a position to receive a total opening of conscience. Furthermore, unlike novice-masters, for example, they do not receive a delegation of the superior's powers for the final discernment. The fact that they are not imposed but at the most suggested, either individually or as members of a group (the teaching staff, for instance), confirms their character as 'consultants'.

From this arises a situation which is at first sight paradoxical: they have access to a person's conscience but remain outside the process of discernment carried out by their hierarchical superiors. Thus their task is made up of two predominating elements: they are at the service of those they direct, and they render this service as consultants.

They are at the service of those they direct—at the same time they are not at their mercy. The moment a priest assumes the task of direction at the implicit or explicit proposal of the candidate he agrees to assist him in the objective search for the authenticity of his call. But he must never go beyond this. It is his duty to confront the candidate with his responsibilities, examine the reasons for his aspirations, follow his development and throw light on his decisions. In short he makes him aware of all the things that go to make up his vocation. Generally the collaboration of director and directed proceeds without any serious tensions or profound disagreements.

If by chance their relations should become strained or impaired, the director should look to see whether his own attitude has anything to do with it. Indeed it may happen that an incompatibility of character, a personal prejudice or a persistent misunderstanding is getting in the way. The best thing to do in that case would be to recommend the one under his direction to go to another director. It may also happen that the fault lies with the person directed. Either he may not accept the real significance of certain unfavourable indications which are not obvious, but are nonetheless serious; or he may refuse to open himself in all simplicity. It is then up to the director to be firm and not let himself be put off by these emotional disturbances. He must stress the necessity of complete frankness and the obligation in conscience which results from major impediments.

Should the one receiving direction not correct himself, he will have to point out to him that he must look for another director, and that he must communicate to him the reasons for the change and the exact bearing of the points being disputed. It may even happen, should he persist in his determination to go on in spite of his unsuitability or serious impediments, that the director must order him, under pain of grave sin, to make known the difficulties to the competent superior.

Fortunately these are exceptional cases, although they are by no means unheard of. It would be certainly culpable to weaken for fear of the reactions of the one being directed. The director would then be exposing the one under direction to the danger of going on when there is no possibility of amendment before the definitive commitment. This leads straight to disaster—*after* this commitment.

The director is at the service of the person he directs, and this service has its own precise and inescapable conditions. He carries out his work as a consultant, and this means that he must make the one directed aware of his responsibilities while under no circumstances acting as a substitute for him.

The decision of the one under direction must remain entirely personal. The priest who directs may not take advantage of his knowledge, his experience, his function or the grace of his state of life to go beyond the task allotted him in the process of discerning a vocation, for by doing so he usurps the rights of the competent superiors and their possible delegates and also deprives the candidate of his liberty, by acting as a substitute for him. All he can do—and this is not as inconsiderable as it may appear—is to help the candidate perceive clearly the movements of grace, so that he may decide with full knowledge of the case and act upon what he knows.

When it comes to the final decision, those responsible for the discernment of vocations are bishops or major superiors, who may call upon the assistance of collaborators. Those who receive delegated authority participate in the ultimate discernment to the extent that their measure of delegation permits. Those who are called in for consultation have no formal participation in it: their conclusions are opinions whose meaning and significance will be fitted by the competent superior into the pattern of facts at his disposal and will motivate his decision.

The candidate, for his part, must make his own attempts at discernment, admittedly tentative and conditional, but no less real for that. He can call for assistance, and in practice it is indispensable that he should do so. Any properly qualified priest can be called on for this purpose. The candidate should give preference to the priests suggested by the superiors, while remaining free to go to others should he wish. These priests have a strict duty to make an objective search for the will of God; in no case may they make themselves accessories to a will which refuses to do its own work, is going astray or is simply blinding itself.

The definitive confirmation comes when the various forms of collaboration we have described converge and come together at one point. The candidate's judgment on religious profession or the priesthood: 'I am called by God and I commit myself' is joined by the judgment of the superior or the bishop: 'He is called and I engage him'. The first judgment is confirmed by the second, and assumed into it. The fusion of these two judgments, made with full knowledge of the case, is the outcome of a lengthy development of grace working both in the individual soul and in the community of the Church.

This it is which gives the vocation as a whole its certainty. All the other forms and preliminary measures are conditional upon it and are only truly valid in so far as they participate in it as provisional means or stages.

CHAPTER III

THE DISCERNMENT OF EXTERNAL VOCATION

DIVINE vocation, which is the immediate object of the work of discernment, presents two aspects which, although complementary, are sufficiently distinct to allow of separate treatment. Consideration will be given first of all to the external graces which combine to form the candidate's aptitude as a whole to the sort of life he has in mind. They can be revealed more easily, observed more conveniently and judged more objectively than internal graces and their effects, and so it is normal to start any investigation from this point.

1. THE MEANING AND IMPORTANCE OF APTITUDES

It should never be forgotten that the presence of the required aptitudes does not constitute a positive sign of internal vocation. This should be kept in mind when dealing with candidates who are very gifted or eminently suitable.

Faced with such a candidate, the occasional adviser and particularly the usual director may easily allow themselves to be carried away by a very understandable but purely human desire—the gain for the diocese, the order or the congregation in securing such a recruit. It would be no small satisfaction for the director to know himself responsible for recruiting such a person.

There is no need whatever to fight shy of a brilliant candidate or to discourage him for fear of doing the wrong thing. The desire to see an exceptionally gifted young man or woman enter the Lord's service is in itself legitimate and to work for it to the best of one's ability is worthy. But we must be honest about it and see whether personal satisfaction and the credit to the body to which we belong play too great a part in our hopes for this particular person.

But let us be under no delusions. The person under direction is sometimes more perspicacious than his director and his later development in religious life will certainly be spoilt if he has noticed, even if only vaguely, that all our enthusiasm was motivated by human calculation rather than submission to the spirit of God.

The qualities and abilities necessary for the making of a good priest, a good religious, or a good regular priest are minimum conditions. The candidate who does not measure up to them can under no circumstances be considered as having a vocation. This is obvious, since God does not contradict himself. But it is not possible to lay down a collection of talents and abilities which shall provide a sure sign of an internal vocation without reducing ordinary Christian people to a sub-human or sub-moral level, or accusing perfectly good Christians of infidelity because they have remained in the world.

In practice it is not infrequent to come across cases in which a person's abilities may be only middling, to say the least, without actually being diriment impediments, but in which there seem to be clear signs of an internal vocation. In the same way it often happens that candidates may, even to an eminent degree, possess all that is needed to make a good priest, except the internal vocation.

To grieve because the former come in and stay in, or because the latter either go away or do not come in at all, is the sign of a mind which refuses to believe in the unpredictable movements of grace or in the ways of the Lord, which are rather different from ours.

It would appear, then, that the study of a candidate's aptitudes is essentially a matter of declaring that there are no serious impediments.

Canon Law proceeds in the same way when it lays down the aptitudes required for admission to minor and major orders. In the first place it lists the minimum conditions for validity (being baptized and of male sex) and for liceity (being in a state of grace, confirmed and of canonical age, leading an upright, moral life and commanding sufficient theological knowledge). Then it passes on to irregularities (impediments which, once incurred, can only be removed by dispensation) and to simple impediments (which can cease on their own and for which it is not necessary to ask for dispensation unless they are still actually present).

If the minimum conditions are fulfilled and no impediment is detected, it may be concluded that aptitude is there, and the candidate can therefore present himself for the reception of orders. It goes without saying that this aptitude—which is met with in so many cases—has no binding effect. It remains to be seen whether he has the internal vocation.

In order to show these aptitudes more clearly something should be said about the main counter-indications, either serious or diriment, which, for the sake of convenience, can be put under three headings generally recognized as valid: bodily health, mental health and spiritual balance.

All the canonical impediments to admission to orders can be placed under these three headings. Since canonical impediments are sanctioned in a particular way by the Church and entail juridical measures, it would be better to say a few words about them first.

In effect it devolves entirely upon the superiors, when admitting candidates, to find out and make sure whether there is any question of irregularity or impediment. And it is also for them alone to ask for a dispensation if, for various reasons, the internal vocation seems likely and so justifies this step.

The priest, however, whether an occasional adviser or regular director, must be informed about the terms of the canonical impediments. These may be irregularities incurred without any personal fault: illegitimate birth, serious deformity, epilepsy or mental illnesses even when they have been cured. They may also be incurred as a result of criminal acts: attempted suicide, murder, taking part in any way whatsoever in an abortion followed by the death of the foetus. They may be simple impediments arising from recent conversion to Catholicism or from the fact that the father is a non-Catholic.

Again, it is very rare for the director or adviser to have to make a definite judgment on these impediments or ask for a dispensation —but it is important that he should stress their significance and the reasons for them, if need be, without giving rise to alarm or aggravating any sense of guilt. A large number of irregularities are contracted without even the slightest personal guilt; others arise from serious guilt, but can be fully forgiven and atoned for. But it is desirable that he should help the person he is directing to see these impediments in the order of providence. They are the expression of God's will and as such form a part in the discernment of vocations on the level of aptitudes.

Another category of impediments must be mentioned here. It is closely related to that of Canon Law. Certain religious congregations, like certain dioceses, have erected their own duly established impediments.

A congregation of nuns may have taken the impediment of illegitimate birth from Canon Law. A particular order may not admit candidates who have already been members of another religious order. A certain diocese may provide that some grave sexual offences (e.g. full sexual relationship with a woman, even if on only one occasion) should entail exclusion.

It is hardly likely that a director would be fully informed about all these particular measures, and in many cases it would even be impossible for him to obtain detailed information about them all. Probably this is not even really necessary. If the director remains aware of the part he has to play, which is to dispose the candidate to open himself wholly to the will of God, no harm is done in leaving the final decision to the superiors.

The discernment of vocations before the actual entry is always conditional upon a later ratification. The candidate who has learnt to look on his vocation as a response to an objective appeal will not be baffled should some such obstacle present itself, but will see in it a providential indication which falls naturally into the spiritual attitude he has towards vocation. These impediments which attach to individual religious congregations are a timely reminder that the discernment carried out by the priest must be inspired by an accurate idea of his 'disposing' rôle.

Consideration can now be given to the defects which may reveal themselves under the three headings already given: bodily health, mental health and spiritual equilibrium.

2. PHYSICAL HEALTH

Bodily health might be thought the easiest to define. Serious illnesses and obvious infirmities for which treatment is required before admission are quickly spotted. A doctor will be called in for doubtful cases and, in the present state of medical science, he will have at his disposal an imposing array of means by which he can give a firm diagnosis.

Experience, however, shows that in practice the problems set by a precarious or none too robust state of health are both numerous and varied. Even with the assistance of skilled physicians superiors often find themselves confronted by distressing decisions. For this reason it is desirable to look carefully at the attitude to be taken before entry by priest, by doctor consulted and by superior.

The rôle of the priest consulted before entry

Any priest consulted by a candidate who does not complain of any serious indisposition or bodily infirmity may encourage him to present himself to the superiors, if an internal vocation seems in other respects probable. It is sufficient for him to point out that it is up to the superior later to prescribe a medical examination.

But the priest should bear in mind that the presence of an illness does not necessarily lead to the conclusion that there is definitely no internal vocation. This is obvious for a state of health which is only temporarily impaired, and it applies also to incurable illness, even serious ones. Indeed health requirements differ from congregation to congregation, and are an expression of their way of life and the nature of their ministries. It should not be forgotten that there are congregations for sick people in which robust health is an 'impediment' to admission! There are others in which invalid candidates will be accepted to live together with members in good health.

All the same, the priest will do well to mention at the very start the hazard which sickness represents. Superiors know that it often has important psychological repercussions which are an even greater obstacle to religious life than the sickness itself.

Furthermore the priest must realize that many candidates form a wrong idea of the state of health required for the type of life they have in mind. The contemplative life, for instance, normally demands even more robust physical health than the active life. It is useful, not to say necessary, to dispel any illusions on this point. The candidate's desires may not permit him to judge objectively whether he is strong enough to endure fasts, privations and other penances. Without discouraging him it is necessary to bring him to view the question clearly and convince him that it is for the superiors to make a judgment. Actually involved as they are in the life which they represent, superiors really do know just what demands it makes. Moreover, when they meet with a doubtful case they will turn to a doctor.

The specific task of the doctor and the responsibilities of superiors

What sort of doctor should be approached? It is desirable that he should be a good Catholic. It is even more imperative that he should be a competent doctor. But it is of supreme importance that he should be really well informed about the type of life for which the candidate is preparing himself.

What, in fact, is asked of him is not merely to reach a full and accurate diagnosis. He must be able to give some idea of a sick person's reactions to the demands, effort and strains which will be imposed by a certain way of life in certain surroundings. His diagnosis must be complimented by a prognosis taking into account the sort of life the candidate is likely to be leading. Without this, his opinion, although perfectly correct, will not be of much use. One and the same form of heart trouble will take on a different significance for a monk and a missionary out in the bush; and the same weakness of health will not entail the same effects for an enclosed nun and a nursing or teaching sister.

Unfortunately the ever growing number of 'special branches' in medicine tends to favour the fragmentary diagnosis. It is worth asking whether there is not room for a special effort to find competent doctors who, by regular contact with a particular type of life, might be in a better position to speak authoritatively about such cases and to arrive at a really complete and useful opinion. It would be desirable also for these doctors—either on their own or in collaboration with specialist colleagues—to be able to estimate disturbances and indispositions of psychological origin.

Medical assistance of this sort would perform a great service for superiors. As things are at present they are often just as much at a loss after the consultation as before. It is not surprising that some of them become so sceptical that they only call for a medical diagnosis when they want to get rid of a candidate for completely different reasons. Bodily health is a useful maid of all work, and no one can feel hurt when such an objective reason is given! This, unfortunately, turns into a mere caricature of the discernment of vocations. There is, in fact, good and increasing reason to pay serious attention to medical consultation, particularly when it is not cut off from the question of mental health.

The dissatisfaction felt with much medical diagnosis may well come from the fact that the general practitioner is being faced with problems which he is not always in a good position to solve. He is often consulted about so-called minor indispositions: headaches, insomnia, stomach pains, constipation, diarrhoea, etc., and it is normal to call upon him for such help. These are evidently symptoms of a somatic nature. When their origin is finally located (sinusitis, heart trouble, bilious disorders, liver complaints, etc.), suitable medical treatment is applied, and if necessary an operation is performed. The fact that the symptoms disappear proves that they have been cured and therefore that the diagnosis was correct.

Sometimes, however, such interventions have no effect; sometimes the improvement is scarcely noticeable or only temporary. And quite often the doctor may even decide against any intervention because 'there is nothing wrong'.

This assertion must be understood properly. From the somatic point of view, which is that of the great majority of doctors, even specialists, it is correct. The examination has revealed no cause which the doctor can put right. But it would be wrong to assume that the symptoms are imaginary. The fact that no explanation is to be found at the somatic level is not an occasion for doing nothing. All the indications are for going further and finding out whether the cause may not lie in the psychological order. The unity of man's composite nature means that there is nothing new-fangled or shocking about such a supposition.

It has always been acknowledged that 'feelings' or 'states of mind' affect the functionings of the organism. The effects are very noticeable. Anger makes the blood rush to the head, sometimes even bringing about an apoplexy; fear paralyses, grips people in the pit of the stomach and makes it impossible to close one's eyes; sadness destroys the appetite; shock makes one go cold; disgust turns the heart over; tension causes headaches. All these images of everyday speech express an intimate experience of the unity of our being. The enormous progress of somatic medicine has tended over the years to make the somatic aspect of illness an almost exclusive preoccupation, while the psychological aspects have remained in the background.

Prescribing tranquillizers, narcotics, laxatives or vitamins is useful for passing indispositions. With the help of these treatments the psychosomatic balance is restored and the trouble disappears. But there is a danger of making the troubles worse if these prescriptions are kept up over a course of years in that they do not attack the real causes which are given a chance to build up slowly but surely. To neutralize them it would be necessary to increase the doses, not without serious and distressing consequences. When the crisis suddenly comes, it is all the more difficult to handle because of the length of time it has had to prepare itself.

The superior has a duty to himself to take minor indispositions, which do not make it necessary for a person to keep to his bed or room, seriously. If the doctor affirms that there is nothing wrong when headaches, stomach-aches and indigestion pains go on for months and even years, he must take this opinion for what it means: there is nothing wrong that the doctor has been able to discover or put right.

It may be nothing, as far as somatic medicine is concerned, but this is certainly not true for the sufferer, who certainly does have something wrong with him. The usual remarks will be made: imaginary headaches exist only in the head of the doctor or the superior, or of anyone else who makes out that he is suffering from headaches or stomach-aches when there is really nothing wrong with him at all. Anyone who suffers like this is certainly sick in the head ... It is important to be logical about all this and to call in specialists, equipped and trained to discover causes which are not of the somatic order, to make a diagnosis in these particular fields, suggest suitable treatment and estimate the possible repercussions.

Somatic medicine is indispensable and performs outstanding services: it is not to be dismissed out of hand. But it is not everything. To assuage the sufferer by prescribing remedies which certainly relieve the pain, but which the doctor himself does not put much faith in, is no solution and may become harmful.

When priests or mature religious, after ten or twenty years of priestly or religious life, come to complain of pains which they find unbearable, it is most unusual if they have not already consulted one or more doctors about the significance of these warning signs. Sure of his real but limited knowledge, the doctor has told them that nothing is wrong ... Somewhat surprised, but relieved, the superiors have re-affirmed that nothing is wrong ... Resigned to the inevitable or glad not to have anything to worry about, they have told themselves that nothing is wrong. And then suddenly from this accumulation of nothings there arises the crisis which prostrates them or the deep-seated illness which torments them. Only then does anyone wonder whether psychological factors have anything to do with the case and a specialist is called in for examination. It is hardly surprising that it takes two or three years to cure what has been building up over ten or twenty.

In practice the following course could be followed. First of all consult the general practitioner or family doctor. If the indisposition persists refer to a specialist in one field or other of somatic medicine. If their combined efforts reveal 'nothing', thank them for their services, for they have done their job thoroughly and well. It will then be necessary to turn to doctors who are able to discover the psychological causes.★

★ Regular mention is made of medical specialists. It would be advisable, therefore, once for all, to set down clearly the special branches of medicine which can be met with.

Although somatic medicine has many branches, they can be recognized easily enough by the names they bear. These refer either to techniques practised or to the organs of parts of the body which are treated. In addition to the general practitioner, everyone has heard of the surgeon, the radiologist and the obstetrician. There are also the dermatologist (skin diseases), the ophthalmologist (eyes), the stomatologist (mouth), and the ear, nose and throat specialist. Among doctors concerned with internal medicine (diseases of internal organs: heart, lungs, stomach, liver, intestines, kidneys, etc.), the special branches become more and more varied. The gynaecologist has been familiar for a long time, but now increasing reference is made to the cardiologist, chest physician, specialist in liver diseases, urologist, endocrinologist, etc.

Neurology is also a special branch of somatic medicine since it is concerned with studying diseases of the nervous system, i.e. lesions which occur and various troubles such as palsies, spasms, etc. Since the nervous system also comprises the higher centres such as the brain, it is not surprising that the neurologist should be confronted with certain lesions (e.g. tumours on the brain) which entail psychological disturbances.

The psychiatrist differs from all the specialists mentioned in that he devotes himself to the study of mental (or psychological) illness. Classical psychiatry discerns and studies these illnesses in the symptoms or syndromes (i.e. characteristic patterns or groups of symptoms) which they reveal. It attempts to assess the probable development of these morbid states and to find a suitable course of treatment.

It may perhaps be objected that such specialists are rare, and this is true. But what is at stake is sufficiently important to take the trouble to locate them. They do exist, and very good ones at that. Some of them even work in concert with priests, and in this

---

During the last fifty years the so-called dynamic psychiatry has attempted to go a step further and make out the psychic structures characteristic of each of these illnesses. While not denying the possibility of somatic causes, it aims to establish these structures by looking at the human psyche as a whole—and the pictures formed differ very greatly in the various schools of depth psychology. That these schools and theories should be so numerous is by no means surprising. Unlike somatic medicine, in fact, they cannot refer to organs or parts of the body which can be objectively revealed, but find themselves forced to infer what the general structure of the psyche is by patient observation and careful cross-checking.

While these problems were being studied it was confirmed that many somatic indispositions and disturbances (e.g. asthma, ulcers, colitis, hypertension, skin complaints, etc.) assumed a significance within some of these psychic structures. The main purpose of psycho-somatic medicine is to discover the psychological significance of these somatic manifestations in order to provide adequate remedies for these complaints.

The aim of psychotherapy is to help those suffering from mental illness. Going from a knowledge of psychic structures it tries by appropriate methods to re-establish equilibrium which is in danger of being lost. By preference it applies itself to neuroses, which are revealed by anxieties, phobias, obsessions, etc., without, however, the judgment and sense of reality of the patient having been fundamentally impaired. It can also be carried out for psychoses (mental illnesses in the strict sense), but here its application is much more difficult because, by definition, the judgment and sense of reality of the patients are profoundly disturbed.

It should be noted finally that in certain cases specialized branches are joined together: e.g. the neuro-psychiatrist, the psychotherapeutic neuro-psychiatrist, etc.

All these designations so far mentioned, are more or less officially recognized. The boundaries of each are generally accepted. But the expression 'nervous illnesses' remains ambiguous. Many doctors whose orientation and training are quite different—psychiatrists, neurologists, psychotherapists, etc.—make use of it because it does not alarm their patients. But for objective information about each doctor's specialized field, more experience and training is required.

way they are able to take religious factors into account, for although every minor, but persistent, indisposition is of considerable significance, it is not necessarily a sign that a vocation is lacking. Far from it: it may well go hand in hand with an authentic call from God. With this knowledge, reticence or hesitation may be disregarded at the time of admission. Such things are curable if given adequate attention; otherwise they will, in time, create serious handicaps, if not unbearable ills.

It is obvious that in all these cases psychological factors must be taken into account. This is why a few comments under our second heading, mental health, will throw light upon what somatic medicine may describe as 'nothing'.

3. MENTAL HEALTH

In defining what mental health means it is essential to clear away all misunderstanding. We are not concerned with the soul, the vital principle of the philosophers, the spiritual principle of the theologians. By the psyche we mean the totality of structures and dynamisms which are not strictly organic, while at the same time they are not strictly spiritual. It should not be considered as an entity apart, nor made into a pure abstraction. The psyche is a region of human existence whose often bewildering complexity is never without its own unity. This region has its own characteristics; it is governed by its own particular laws, and it requires to be investigated by appropriate methods. Psychology, with its expanding network of individual disciplines, is devoted to studying it.

The psyche is no more a static entity than the body is.

It possesses fundamental attributes, whose absence is rightly considered abnormal. These are the primordial impulses which every human being has, by nature. It is subject to growth, which progresses at a flexible, but ordered, pace. A stoppage of, or a deviation from, this flexible rhythm, is pathological. It ends in a mobile yet stable equilibrium. Fixation or instability are signs of death or deterioration.

We may term mental health that condition where we find adequate structures of growth, having regard to the age of the individual under consideration. Mental health is disturbed by over-attachment to particular matters (fixation), by blockages (inhibitions), by reverting to an earlier stage (regression), by failure to make progress (infantilism, immaturity), by disordered and uncontrolled urges (imbalance). This is by no means the whole gamut of possible psychological ills.

It is desirable that the candidate to the religious or priestly life should enjoy good physical health, and even more so that his mental health should be good. The psyche, being more closely linked with the spiritual and supernatural, can the more easily stand in their way. It is therefore urgently necessary to recognize symptoms in this field, but we can meet with very real difficulties in the process.

For centuries this sort of discernment has been purely empirical. It should not be thought that it has at any time been non-existent. From the very earliest times—and the writings of the Fathers of the Church and the Desert Fathers bear this out—attention has always been paid to it. In various formulations which seem anti-quated to us is hidden a fund of experience built on common sense and careful observation: 'Is he of good character? Is he petulant, artful or restless? Is he given to exaltation or over-enthusiasm? Is he resourceful, full of initiative and high spirits? Is he peevish or morose? Is he fantastical? Are his moods stable or mercurial? etc.'. The experience of centuries handed down from generation to generation, together with personal perspicacity, enabled superiors to form judgments in good faith and with an untroubled conscience. They probably did not go much more widely astray than our own professional psychologists.

But for about sixty years things have been changing. The mushroom growth of psychologies—for they are legion—have brought about an indefinable but persistent uneasiness. The fault does not lie so much in the psychologies themselves, which are respectable and serious sciences, even if some of their initiates are given to rather extreme ideas; but the same cannot be said for the popularizers by whom the public at large has been fed with sensational elements, with no attempt made to set these elements in their true context or to give any details about their real significance. These innumerable popularizations have opened at our very feet giddy abysses. They have cast a harsh and pitiless light on things which had only been mentioned in a low voice and in veiled terms. Wherever they go they uncover incestuous or parricidal desires. They see complexes in everything. They are forever running across inhibitions. All values hitherto held sacred—civilization, morality, religion—have been reduced to the level of false and inconsistent sublimations. The less one knows, the more one is taken in.

This leads to a paradoxical situation in which people know too much to avoid anxiety, and yet too little to be able to cope with this anxiety. They are conscious of the need to know more and yet of a fear of probing too far. Superiors and directors constantly meet cases in which they detect some pathological feature, but for want of thorough knowledge they neither dare nor are able to form any judgment. It need not be wondered that uncertainty paralyzes them. Yet uncertainty can have more disastrous consequences for those entrusted to their care than a short and summary judgment. Superiors hesitate before cases which definitely are pathological because they have heard tell how frequent these are; and they confuse frequency with normality. Yet, on the other hand, certain transitory crises may rouse them to draconian measures because they have heard descriptions of the frightful sequels of such crises and thus confuse a crisis attendant on growth with a permanent state.

Systematic examination before entry

Since psychology has achieved the status of an independent science, it seems only reasonable to turn to qualified specialists for the examination of mental health. These specialists would tackle in their own field the same task as doctors consulted about bodily health.★

It is possible in this context to foresee some sort of 'systematic' examination, with all candidates being asked to go and see the specialist, who, with the collaboration of colleagues if necessary, would try to discover any diriment symptoms or any defects to be adjusted. His conclusions would be submitted to the superior who, in accord with the candidate, would be able to take the measures required.†

★ Article 33 of the *Statuta Generalia,* which are a continuation of the Apostolic Constitution *Sedes Sapientiae,* provides explicitly, in addition to the examination of physical health, for the establishing of candidates' psychological aptitude by calling in a competent doctor for advice based on a judicious history and diagnosis ('*adhibito quoque probati medici anamnestico et diagnostico diligenti iudicio*').

† Systematic examination before entry is everywhere still at a more or less experimental stage, and for this reason specialists wisely continue to be very reserved in their publications. The reader who wants to learn more about experiments made or being made should consult the following works:

An article by Père D. H. Salman, O.P. (*Le discernement des vocations religieuses,* Supplement of *Vie Spirituelle,* no. 52, 1960, pp. 81-98) lists the principal techniques which may be applied and shows their scope and limitations. Another, by W. Bier, S.J. (*L'examen psychologique, ibid.,* no. 29, 1954, pp. 118-151), describes the experiment made by the author in the United States and gives some details about the method he followed. Th. N. MacCarthy (*L'investigation psychologique de la personnalité dans l'examen des vocations religieuses, ibid.,* no. 54, 1960, pp. 340-50)

There are various ways of carrying out such an examination. A single specialist could be made responsible for studying the psychological aspects as such. The examination might also be entrusted to a psychiatrist, who would be more likely to know incipient signs of eventual mental illness; or to a priest, one well-informed about psychology and even better informed about the spiritual psychology of vocation. Such a priest, working with the specialists, would normally be in a better position to discern the probable impact of psychological deficiencies. The information available to the superior could only gain in objectivity from this course.

In some countries, teams like this (comprising a psychiatric-psychologist and a priest, or perhaps a psychologist, a psychiatrist and a priest) have been formed. Their pioneering work has enabled the most satisfactory features to be selected. Experience shows that the system will function best given three conditions: that these consultations are presented in the right way to the candidates; that each adviser is quite clear about the scope of the task allotted him; and that the exact terms of professional secrecy are defined. These three points must be considered in greater detail.

It is a good thing for the superior himself to explain to the

---

refers to the same facts as the previous writer to examine the possibilities for the psychologist in these fields and to determine the most effective methods. L. Beirnaert, S.J., in a very acute and carefully balanced contribution (*L'investigation psychanalytique des candidats, ibid.*, no. 53, 1960, pp. 179-186), describes what the psychoanalyst can do by his own particular methods in the discernment of vocations. Finally an article by Père A. Plé, O.P. (*Une expérience du discernement des vocations, ibid.*, no. 56, 1961, pp. 75-91) gives an excellent glimpse of the work done by a team consisting of a priest, an analytic psychiatrist and clinical psychologist, who receive all the candidates of an order before entry.

The study by Père A. Benkö and Prof. J. Nuttin gives numerous details about the tests used. It should, however, be noted that this study was made on candidates already in religious life and that, since this book appeared, it has been discontinued, Father Benkö having left for South America after defending his thesis at Louvain.

candidate the reasons for taking this step, pointing out that it is not inspired by any misgivings about him or intended to extract secrets from him; that the specialists are there to help him to see more clearly and to allow the superior to carry out his responsibilities more fully; that the whole procedure is part of the objective search for the will of God. Experience gives ample proof that candidates, if judiciously informed, are quite ready to accept the reasons for an examination of this kind.

The specialist is brought in as a consultant, to advise on psychical aptitudes and their implications. His rôle is at all points parallel to that of the doctor judging physical aptitude, and thus he would be exceeding it were he to venture to tell a candidate that he lacked a vocation. Where necessary, he must indicate the psychic defects or disturbances, explain their repercussions and propose some remedy or therapy. All these points must be made absolutely clear before any candidate is sent to the specialist, and superiors and specialists should together work out how far the consultation should go; otherwise serious misunderstandings may arise from which the candidate himself, and often the whole religious community, will suffer. Occasion should also be taken to set beforehand the exact terms of professional secrecy.

The consultant is bound by professional secrecy, and without the consent of the person consulting him he cannot impart to a third party anything he has learnt, either directly or indirectly, during the interviews. Since this is a strict obligation with a view to the common good, the specialist may not consider himself dispensed simply because he is dealing with a candidate to the priestly or religious life. And so it is necessary to obtain the candidate's unreserved consent beforehand—does he agree that the specialist may inform the superior of his findings? When the consent has not been asked for in advance, it will be necessary to proceed with great circumspection should these findings ever need to be made known. One could explain to the candidate—and this time the task belongs to the consultant—the usefulness of imparting to the superior the conclusions reached in the interviews. Or one might explain the advantages of a discussion between the specialist and the superior or director, if necessary in the presence of the candidate, and ask for his consent. In all this tact, prudence and, above all, honesty, are needed. It would be very harmful for the candidate to get the impression that he has been betrayed or led into a trap. His freedom must remain intact. Experience, indeed, has shown that honesty alone pays. The human approach which respects the person and disdains all subterfuge contributes greatly towards creating a favourable atmosphere of confidence. It is on points like this that the priest member of the team can make his contribution. His priestly ministry and his own personal contact with the ideal which the candidate has set before himself both mark him out as a mediator.

The examination of doubtful cases during formation

If such particulars are observed, then the examination of the mental health of every candidate will indisputably contribute towards more judicious selection. But unfortunately the number of skilled specialists is unavoidably still very restricted, since this is so recent a science. Even superiors who wish to make this their general practice sometimes find themselves forced to give up the idea for lack of qualified collaborators.

This should not cause too great a concern. Candidates can be admitted to the noviciate or seminary in accordance with the usual norms, only those being sent for examination who, either at the outset or during the course of their years of formation, remain doubtful cases. As there are so few of these, it will be easier to find a specialist who will agree to come and see them, and even to undertake a long journey if need be. The trouble would be well worth while.

Examination before entry certainly has one advantage: candidates who are obviously unsuitable and will be a useless burden and even a vexation to the community can be eliminated and this avoids young people having to leave the house of formation after trying it for one or two years, if not longer, even though they were sooner or later bound to give up. But an examination made during formation offers surer guarantees. Since the candidate is older, immaturity will be more clearly in evidence and can be more decisively confirmed. Since he has been leading the life he chose out for himself, reactions and deficiencies are more revealing. Thus an examination carried out during the years of formation can be more conclusive and result in a more clear-cut recommendation, especially if a psychiatric psychologist conducts the examination in collaboration with a competent priest. This is the only sort of collaboration which offers the possibility of the right sort of recommendation, with reference to the whole range of medical, psychological and spiritual aspects and their interaction on each other. As we will see later, in practice it is not possible to discern internal vocation with any finality before entry. This is why systematic examination before admission is negative (elimination of unsuitable candidates and those unlikely to improve), while examination after several years of formation is positive (confirmation of those whose vocation, both external and internal, offers worthwhile guarantees). These practical advantages incline many specialists to prefer the latter to a systematic examination before entry. In both cases the same method of presenting such an examination to the candidate, defining the task of each specialist and coming to an understanding about professional secrecy, should be followed.*

★ In several countries teams of a more or less permanent nature have been formed which undertake to examine doubtful cases during the years of formation. Some of them have been recognized, explicitly or implicitly, by the diocesan or religious authorities. Generally these teams are made up of a specialist priest and a psychiatrist (who is often also a psychotherapist); they are sometimes joined by a psychologist.

The present writer is a member of one such team, which has laid down a programme which is submitted to the superior and the candidate for agreement before the examination is undertaken. For the sake of further information the text of it is reproduced here.

PSYCHO-RELIGIOUS EXAMINATION OF VOCATION

Aim: To provide the competent authorities, who have to decide whether to retain or dismiss a seminarist or young religious, with a detailed opinion based on factors both specifically religious and medicopsychological, and at the same time to promote in the candidate awareness of the nature of a vocation as well as of his own personal difficulties, so that the superiors and the candidate may come, if possible unanimously, to a decision which makes allowance for all the factors at work.

Method: The examination is made by a priest, trained in both spirituality and psychology, and a doctor who is also a psychiatrist and psychotherapist. The two advisers have, separately, two interviews of about an hour with the candidate, with the aim of obtaining details about the following points in particular:

1 General behaviour (in his family and social background as well as in the seminary or religious house) in so far as it provides indications about behaviour later on.

2 Psychic factors and character structures which may, favourably or unfavourably, influence the candidate's life as a religious or priest.

3 General psychic maturity.

4 General religious maturity.

5 The motivation underlying the vocation.

The doctor, if he thinks fit, may call for certain physical examinations or psychological tests.

After the two interviews the advisers separately draw up a detailed written report on their conclusions. These reports are compared and then combined into a single opinion for the competent authorities, who will impart its full implications to the candidate. If any uncertainty remains the advisers will have a third interview with the candidate or ask for a specialized examination as a check, before drawing up the final report.

Professional secrecy: The candidate freely accepts the examination, and thereby undertakes to speak quite openly with the advisers, who may communicate to one another any elements of use for the final report. This is drawn up in such a way that no confidential fact is mentioned without the explicit consent of the candidate.

The final opinion: The definitive report constitutes an opinion, the detailed reasons for which are stated as clearly as possible (in non-technical

Many superiors are still fearful: they express doubts about a candidate's reaction to such a suggestion.

They can set their minds at rest. If the consultation is presented not as an irritating or coercive measure—and so often it is used first as a threat to the recalcitrant or rebellious—but simply as an aid to discernment, then usually no resistance is met with. Several candidates who have been examined have themselves admitted what relief they found it: their difficulties were at last being taken seriously, and, far from frightening them, the consultation gave them new heart.

However, should a candidate refuse to be examined the superior

---

language), but which leaves the final decision to the authorities, who alone are in a position to retain or dismiss a candidate. This definitive report is discussed with nobody. Should, however, the need be felt, it may be presented in detail to the superiors (before their decision) or to the candidate (after the superiors' decision).

Possible psychotherapy after the examination: On principle no psychotherapy is undertaken by the advisers; this is to avoid any distortion of the examination, on the part either of the candidate or the advisers, by the prospect of eventual psychotherapeutic contact.

If for exceptional reasons of a practical nature such therapy is demanded from one of the advisers and undertaken by him, the following line of conduct is to be followed, so that clear emphasis is laid on the difference between the conditions of the therapy and those of the examinations:

1 The decision about therapy being undertaken by one of the advisers is taken by the authorities, without any suggestion on the part of the advisers.

2 A possible examination later on—after the treatment or after a lapse of time fixed beforehand—must be undertaken by a different adviser from the one who advises treatment.

3 Before agreeing to treat a candidate he has examined, the adviser approached must have an interview with this candidate in order to examine whether or not there are any means of going over to therapeutic conditions without danger. In this interview the adviser must clearly explain the implications of the second point to the candidate.

N.B.—The aims and methods of this examination as well as the terms of professional secrecy are clearly explained to the candidate at the very outset of the interviews.

should put it to him tactfully that if in that case any objective grounds for doubt should arise, he would have no choice but to decide against him. The reason why he is proposing this consultation is because he wants fuller information. Nothing but good can come of it: proper treatment and the possibility of cure.

Sometimes the superior will not manage to get the subject's consent. This is generally a sign of serious immaturity. In this case he must stand firm, for mercy is not the same thing as commiseration. Where there is persistent doubt, commiseration is always disastrous and exposes the candidate, as well as the whole body of which he is a part, to the worst consequences.

Doubtful cases, then, will be submitted to a specialized check. The decision for such a step lies with the superior, and it is up to him to recognize those who need it. It is not asking the impossible to require superiors to do this—they are not required to solve the problems, but merely to be able to judge exactly which cases call for fuller information.

It is a task which can also fall upon the spiritual director. A total lack of spiritual initiative, an obviously immature attitude, a false notion of the religious life, retarded sexual development, anxieties, phobias and many other deficiencies will often be spotted by the director before the superior has any suspicion of them. Then the director must send his charge to the superior, in order to obtain his consent to a psychiatric examination, or to send him directly to the specialist if the superior has already given his consent in principle.

In the latter eventuality the director is acting as a 'delegate'. This runs the risk of creating false situations if he does not make quite clear the double rôle he is thenceforth assuming. To avoid all ambiguity it will be sufficient to bring to the candidate's attention the three following points: that the suggestion is put to him with the agreement in principle of the superior; that the director prefers not to bring the matter before the authorities so long as the consultant's conclusions are not known; and that the subject must undertake to inform the superior of the negative conclusions arrived at through the examination, should there be any.

Criteria for recognizing doubtful cases

In order to help superiors and directors spot the really doubtful cases in which examination is called for we must make some attempt to lay down reliable criteria. These could never be called techniques, for this would presuppose a thorough psychological training. They are drawn from careful observation of the subjects in question, and thus they only require the perspicacity and benevolent attention which we can take for granted in every superior and director.★

We will proceed in two stages. In the first place we will give a description of the two extreme groups in which most of the cases to be examined are found; and we will discuss some of the negative indications whose prolonged persistence calls for attention.

a. Criteria drawn from general behaviour

In any community there will always be some people who draw attention to themselves. An anomalous group if ever there was one. But all its members have one thing in common: complaints about them are continually made to the superior: 'They are not like the others; they make themselves conspicuous; they are loud-mouthed and always criticizing; they are always pushing them-

---

★ Criteria of a more technical nature must certainly not be ignored, but priests who are not specialists are liable to be unable to find their way through them. With their needs in mind, Rev. Fr. A. Godin, S.J., has published a *Petit Guide à l'usage du clergé pour discerner les troubles mentaux* (Brussels, Oeuvres des Tracts, 1961, 40 pp.), which may help them better to understand the causes and the significance of psychic disturbances as well as the terminology usually employed.

selves forward; they tread on other people's toes,' etc., etc.

On the other hand there are those who literally disappear in the crowd. Very few complaints are made about them to the superior; and he, for his part, usually has very little to complain about either, except for a few who are over-scrupulous. And so superiors tend to praise them: 'They never grumble; they are not unruly; they obey without a murmur; they ask what they have to do and take care not to do anything they are not told to do; they say how pleased they are with the general run of things as they are and are quite put out by an unexpected change; they do not approach anyone outside the times appointed by rule,' etc., etc. They seem to ask only one thing: to pass unnoticed.

You may say that the first group are all unbalanced, but this is just not true! Outstanding intelligence, great fervour, artistic gifts or human talents will always make their possessors 'conspicuous'. If people like this can bring to the gifts bestowed on them by their Creator the spiritual values of humility, detachment and charity they will make outstanding priests or religious. They are often difficult during the years of formation and even afterwards, merely because they are above the general run.

Those who make themselves conspicuous through a need to attract attention when nothing justifies it are quite a different matter. They criticize at random and harp on the weak points of others, but with a partiality which borders on insincerity. They swagger and show off. They are high-handed defenders of theories which they do not understand themselves or which ring false. They attack everyone and get worked up about endless, irrelevant controversies. All means seem good to them if they can get what they want.

When a superior or director hears such grievances from their fellows, or from teachers or lesser superiors, he may perhaps be astonished. It is not unknown for such people to appear extremely correct, courteous, obedient, deferential, if not obsequious, particularly towards superiors. Do not be misled. Such ambivalence is more serious than excess which although pronounced is at least consistent.

In the second group also good subjects are often to be found. Grace is working in them, profoundly, but not spectacularly. Their calmness, modesty and patience are genuine. Their containment is due not to fear but to recollection within their own hidden potentialities. They will turn into men of God whose spiritual radiance is moulded from gentleness and kindness.

The suspect cases in this second group are not really showing calm, modesty and patience at all. Their whole attitude is governed by complacency, emptiness or sloth; or they may be haunted by the fear of having to face up to and solve their difficulties. Directors —more so than superiors—quite often receive such people's admissions of their inward distress or witness their emptiness—a distress marked by terror, fatalism and discouragement, an emptiness betrayed by apathy, indolence and lack of will.

The non-genuine cases in both groups are serious. They must be discovered in good time. For what they have been seeking in the priesthood or religious life is above all something to stabilize or compensate themselves. Their boasting or their indolence are only apparent and conceal a gnawing anxiety, which they are instinctively afraid of facing up to.

This is why such people usually oppose the idea of consulting a specialist. Sometimes they express their objections with a disconcerting candour that suggests good faith and leads to the postponement of measures which are indispensable. The first group assert confidently: 'Only perfection will satisfy me!—There is nothing greater than the life of a priest—I would never willingly fall short!' The second murmur plaintively: 'What would I do in the world?—How could I survive among all the dangers and difficulties?—Here at least I am safe, why should I change?—In the world I should only go under altogether!'

So deeply-rooted is their self-centredness that they think their importance is self-evident. Unconsciously they realize that by putting it to the test they will lose all their support and security. This is yet a further reason for pushing them, gently but firmly, towards a minimum of self-commitment, making them see that their claim to be following in the Lord's way is mere self-deception. They should not be accused of duplicity or bad faith. What is wrong with them is more subtle and has them so firmly in its grip that they have become identified with it. All the more reason for not weakening in removing them from a sham ideal.

Apart from these seriously affected subjects there are others who, while they are close to the 'happy medium', are still a cause of anxiety. When trying to estimate their troubles, account should be taken of two series of factors which are also to be found in the more serious cases. They may have a family origin or a personal one.

b. *Negative symptoms of family origin*

No one escapes parental influence. Now parents can fail in many ways without there being any occasion to accuse them of any serious omission or deliberate fault.

There are the nervous, unstable, quarrelsome or scrupulous parents. Their defects are not specifically hereditary: at least there is nothing to prove it genetically. But they impregnate the family atmosphere and make a deep mark on the child's mind. Their children have no models with whom to conform, no certainties to refer to. It is hardly surprising that they in their turn are uncertain, hesitant, distrustful or meticulous.

And then there are parents who are given to drink. By this I do not mean acute alcoholism, which, if present before the birth of the child, affects the development of the foetus and occasions hereditary setbacks. Chronic alcoholism in one of the parents provokes the emotional conflicts we have just been talking about. Indeed the things which make by far the greatest impression on the child are the words, blows and scenes which follow upon the state of drunkenness. All intoxication is due to psychological imbalance, and this particular imbalance entails the most harmful consequences and provokes the most far-reaching repercussions.

Finally there are the disunited parents. Their disunion does not have to be finalized by divorce to be damaging. It may often lie concealed under the outward appearances of a happy life together, or be confined to one particular area of disagreement—religion perhaps. But the children do not fail to notice it and it may make a vivid impression on them. They may try to minimize the facts out of love for their parents and quite often they say: 'I admire my parents: their differences of opinion never gave way to scenes; they never quarrelled in front of us; the few times I came upon them unawares they immediately recovered themselves.' It is not necessary to be a professional psychologist to perceive the constant strain charging the family atmosphere and to guess that the calculated remarks and measured gestures only avoided outbursts by banishing all spontaneity and *joie de vivre*.

Family factors are not, however, conclusive on their own. Their mere presence cannot lead to any definite conclusions. They have perhaps imposed a more than usual strain or made things unnecessarily difficult, without actually disturbing the psyche. Individual cases must be judged on their merits, with the realization that only a vigorous and healthy reaction can ward off serious consequences. If the subject does not show any certain signs of a personally attained balance and maturity (his age being taken into account), it would be wise to suspect the possibility of the troubles breaking out afresh.

c. *Negative symptoms of personal origin*

The negative symptoms resulting from personal behaviour can

all be definitely traced back to a more or less far-reaching immaturity. But this immaturity tends to manifest itself in certain particular points. Without making the list too extensive, we can indicate the main contexts in which they occur.

An excessive dependence on environment is revealed in certain people by bitter complaints or petty recriminations: 'No one ever helps me. Other people aren't very kind. They never tell me anything. They only think of me when they want me to do something for them or when they have unpleasant jobs for me.' They pretend to be disappointed by other people's selfishness, although their grievances all the time suggest most strongly a preoccupation with themselves. With others, however, there is a spirit of independence which borders on rebellion. They want to change the whole system from top to bottom and try to do so by carping at everything that is done. A closer look reveals that all their plans are illusions and their words hollow. Obsessed deep down by insecurity, they construct nothing. Excessive dependence and revolutionary independence both equally undermine any co-operation or common effort. People like this demand to be left alone, for they have no fixed rule to go by; yet at the same time they complain bitterly at not receiving any support, because they are afraid of solitude. Yet not for a moment do they have any doubts about themselves, and they invariably blame their disappointments and setbacks on others.

In the emotional sphere immaturity is often evident. It is normal for seminarists and young religious from about eighteen to twenty-two to become sharply aware of the emotional solitude which celibacy inevitably entails. It is then that friendship can raise problems. They feel instinctively that they are running the risk of throwing overboard one of the most precious of human values if they refuse themselves to others, and yet they also realize in a confused way that they must seek and find a substitute for human love. This gives rise to disturbance and insecurity. It is all a part of the normal process of growth, even if in certain cases the distress is very great. The calmness with which superiors and directors listen to such problems will gradually bring the young people to a more adult attitude. Others, however, try to find a sister-soul, or worse still a sort of mother or father figure. They fix their choice upon a superior or director whom they would like to have at their mercy so that he may shoulder all their responsibilities. Or they pour themselves into attachments with their contemporaries, from whom they demand in return an exclusive friendship. When they do not succeed in their attempts at monopoly they go round feeling abandoned, sulk at everyone and brood in their corner, unless their jealousy breaks out in childish bickerings or violent scenes. It need not be stressed that such cases are serious examples of infantilism.

A third sphere in which immaturity comes out easily to the surface is that of sexuality. Immaturity here takes two forms: fascination and prohibition. Fascination is betrayed by thoughts, feelings and physical reactions which take the form of obsession or a fixed idea. Prohibition is shown by an obstinate refusal to consider sexuality or anything to do with it as a human reality. In the first case, they live under the terror of things which everywhere surround them and lie in wait for them; in the second, they are haunted day and night by the fear of ghosts—sexual ones, of course. The combination of these two aspects can be observed in those who are afraid of the instinctive urges they feel and from which they guard themselves as well as they can, without succeeding in ridding themselves of them. Each time they pass from the dejection of defeat to brace themselves for another effort. With all those we are considering, the fear of sexual realities prevents them from seeing clearly. They have not been told sufficiently early of the positive meaning of sexuality as an expression of a full human love inscribed in man's nature by the Creator. And so they are alarmed at the slightest reactions—otherwise quite normal—of their sexual nature; unconsciously they see sin not in acquiescing in what they have sacrificed deliberately, but in the very appearance in their thoughts, feelings and organism of what is an integral part of their nature. Instead of looking calmly at a tendency which of itself is neither vile nor sinful, they feel ashamed of themselves and are driven to distraction. Any victory they think they have won remains illusory and turns into defeat. The more they fight, the more deeply involved they become. The current which could have taken them along quietly soon turns into a quagmire in which they become more and more bogged down in their attempts to struggle free.

These do not exhaust the possibilities, but they are characteristic situations and by no means rare. It should not be assumed immediately that, where such a description seems to fit, the candidate is definitely unsuitable; but the intervention of a really experienced priest or of a medical specialist is called for. When the subject is not too handicapped, four or five well conducted interviews will be able to break the vicious circle which imprisons him. Once released from its grip he will have new courage and strength and be able to go forward with a clear mind. If the case is more serious the specialist must see whether it is a permanent condition or a remediable situation; and if it can be put right he will propose a suitable therapy. In this way the superior or director will be able to take the necessary steps.

Since the specialist's advice is indispensable and courses of treatment, even short ones, presuppose adequate training, there is no need here to give a lengthy description which in any case would be of very little value on account of the necessary technicality. It is hoped that the indications provided will help the superior in his essential work of recognizing those cases for which professional help is required.

Finally it is worth noting that none of the symptoms listed are ever of any significance unless considered in relation to the whole of the individual's psychological constitution. Thus they are only diriment when they are there in addition to, or as a sign of, warped tendencies of long standing. A curable immaturity, overcome by adequate treatment, should not give rise to any fears for the future: the danger of any relapse is negligible. If, on the other hand, such negative symptoms disappear in the course of time, or at entry to the noviciate or seminary, without the candidate having made any personal decision about them, the chances of their reappearing are considerable. As fortune would have it, the reappearance may not happen until immediately after admission to the priesthood or final vows.

4. SPIRITUAL EQUILIBRIUM

Psychological aptitudes have been dealt with at some length, and rightly so. The investigation of the psyche by specific and scientifically valid methods is a recent development, and it was fitting to underline its importance and secure a clear idea of it. But there is always the danger of becoming infatuated with it, and a word should therefore be said about the spiritual faculties of intelligence and will. The quantitative aspect is generally considered among psychological activities. But although in their exercise they are closely bound up with psychological dispositions, in their essence they are quite distinct.

Here, more than anywhere else, it is necessary to distinguish in order to unite. If they receive separate treatment, this is not to make them into abstract and rarified entities. They are not situated in some remote corner of the human person or in some ethereal region far from the influences of the organism and the psyche. Yet these influences are not determining ones: bodily health, even when accompanied by psychological health, does not guarantee the right use of intelligence and will; and likewise certain intellectual or volitional defects do not in themselves warp spiritual vigour.

Some attention, therefore, should be paid to the demands made on candidates by a vocation. It should not be forgotten that the spiritual faculties are considered here as constitutive elements of human existence. The action of grace will not be treated explicitly until the next chapter.

A lucid intelligence

To obtain an idea of a candidate's intelligence it is not sufficient to look at his academic attainments. Many young people get good results in classical studies because they memorize easily: they store up more than they ever assimilate. Others reach a medium standard, but not without straining their powers almost excessively. Some students have very real success at university thanks to their encyclopedic knowledge while remaining at a loss when it comes to the understanding of personal experiences in their lives. Their knowledge of principles is no help to them in practical application.

All this explains why young people coming first in their sixth forms often cut a paltry figure at university, and why others, finishing their university studies with distinction fall down lamentably in later life. The opposite may happen also. A person who does not stand out from the solid but undistinguished mass may show himself later on, particularly when he must act on his own initiative, to possess a seriousness, penetration and originality which had hitherto been quite unexpected.

When it comes to judging aptitude to priestly or religious life, even the most brilliant results should not be allowed to weigh too heavily. Nor should there be too great severity towards the honest medium. There are standard requirements—quite minimal, in fact —from the point of view of present and future studies, but these differ greatly according to the form of life envisaged.

The question, however, which must always be asked is whether the candidate is gifted with an intelligence which enables him to make sure, sound judgments. Whether he is less well gifted for this particular branch of learning or that, or not philosophically inclined, or without the knack of learning languages, is of secondary importance. Provided he has an objective grasp of problems which present themselves to him, knows his limitations, is willing and able to fill in the gaps by more learning and can think straight. Only those candidates whose intelligence is obtuse, utopian or a sham need be considered as basically unsuitable. A vocation presupposes a sound mind, not a well-filled one.

It is not being suggested that the objective assessment of particular intellectual qualities (verbal, motory and abstract intelligence, or powers of analysis and synthesis) are without value. On the contrary, a 'professional orientation' rationally made undoubtedly increases apostolic efficiency, and any later specialization will be of great advantage. But this comes rather within the sphere of the rational organization within a diocese or religious order, and comes after the discernment of aptitudes to the priestly or religious life.

A virtuous will

If a candidate's intelligence must be 'lucid', his will must be 'virtuous'. Virtue as such is not effected by the intensity of the efforts made, nor by the absence of any difficulty. It is a fact of everyday experience: very often the more violent the efforts, the more ineffective they prove to be. How often can be heard the complaint: I have lost all my will-power, I can't do any more!

The will really manifests itself fully when a person, coming to grips with the complexity of a real situation (even though this may have been a purely intuitive process), sees the exact point at which effort must be applied. Then he achieves the intended result with an appropriate expenditure of energy. A realistic will like this naturally supposes a lucid and acute intelligence, for without it it will wear itself out in frustrated efforts. Those domains which are not directly under the control of the will while still forming part of our being are particularly likely to act as the area of choice in such fruitless struggles.

Even before St Augustine, the Desert Fathers distinguished various stages in every moral act: suggestion, confrontation and the personal act of choice. The suggestion (thought, feeling, propensity, etc.) which arises is in itself involuntary and thus premoral. Confrontation consists of becoming aware of and examining this spontaneous appearance, with a view to making a judgment: whether what has arisen from the depths of a person's being will lead him towards good or evil. Even now it is not yet possible to speak of explicit morality—this only comes about after one has assumed a position, and has acquiesced in what leads to good or to evil.

This threefold distinction, nearly two thousand years old, is too often ignored, even by people who call themselves spiritual. They confuse involuntary suggestion with a personal act of choice and thus deny the confrontation. Distracted or terrorized as the case may be, they strive to suppress 'suggestion' at any cost. They yoke themselves to a senseless, impossible task, striving to stifle any involuntary impulse without even asking where it comes from or what it leads to. Now freedom is not to be found at this level. The will has no validity at this level. Any such effort is doomed to failure. It is vitally important that the will should fearlessly confront anything which is a part of human nature, in order to be able to make it a part of the person's whole attitude to life and give it a right direction, either by accepting it or rejecting it or sacrificing it, according to the state of life assumed. To judge of a candidate's will it is necessary to ask whether he is capable of bringing his efforts to bear at the precise point where they may be most effective.

But this is not all. It is also necessary for him to want to make this effort and to succeed with a certain ease. This is what constitutes virtue.

Here again let us be under no illusions. The facility which comes from the absence of obstacles is just as false as the disordered efforts at sledge-hammering. Virtue in our human condition is a personal acquisition. A man who has always told the truth because the thought of lying has never entered his head has at most a fortunate nature. But there is no guarantee that his attitude will not change when the thought does occur to him. All virtue vanishes when it becomes a reflex.

It goes without saying that repetition gives rise to a reflex. But a reflex is always something which repeats itself in a closed circuit. It supposes, and even demands, that there should be no moment of personal choice. It is precisely here that the virtuous habit (as well as the vicious one) is distinguished from the reflex: it is not conditioned by external causes but an internal act of the whole personality into its inmost depths. This is what confers upon the act its consistency, its solidity and its real human value. A person thereby gives meaning to his act, a meaning which will be realized more and more clearly, for this integration, being made time and again in constantly changing circumstances, becomes enriched by all the experience of the past, which in turn helps it adapt itself to the future. This adaptation to the current situation makes accomplishment easier.

The man who strives to perfect his will by repetition of stereotyped acts gives rise only to tics and manias. These unfortunately abound all too frequently in people who think themselves to be virtuous. True virtue, on the other hand, perfects the will by fashioning it and adapting it to an increasingly sensitive and full-blooded accomplishment because the meaning of its acts gains in depth and stands out more and more clearly.

It can be said, then, that the will as a spiritual faculty can be called healthy only if it can bring itself to bear upon the precise points where its exercise will be effective and if it succeeds in conferring on its acts a meaning which makes its efforts easy.

The discernment of 'spiritual' aptitudes is one of the most delicate of tasks. On the one hand the age of the candidate must be taken into account when examining him; on the other the psychological concomitants must not be forgotten.

The candidate's age is a factor in making a judgment, not because the spiritual faculties are themselves affected by it, but because their full exercise supposes a maturity attained or one well on the way to attainment. For this reason there can hardly be any definite pronouncement about candidates under twenty. Nevertheless it is useful to examine on this point in good time. As long as a candidate is still growing in maturity he can be helped to put right certain attitudes which could become permanent. At about twenty-five the judgment may be definite, but without much hope of improvement if defects are revealed.

The psychological concomitants must also be prudently assessed, especially in order to establish whether the defective working of mind or will springs from deep-seated causes. If this is so, the chances of cure are very small; but if the causes are superficial there are well-founded hopes of rapid correction.

Defects of mind or will are all the more serious in consideration of full spiritual development later on. They endanger all apostolic activity, in the widest sense of the word.

Watchful superiors and directors will be able to recognize the doubtful case. Because of the incidence of psychological factors it is right to call in specialists to give their opinion on the seriousness of these draw-backs. But false hopes should not be allowed to pacify real doubts. A mind or will which is not very sound or healthy will not improve with time—on the contrary. Any eccentric, excessive, strange or disconcerting turn of mind will become increasingly marked. Such characteristics often reveal dangerous possibilities, even before any serious deviations have appeared.

The domain of spiritual faculties—which, as has been said, is distinct from the supernatural domain—requires superiors and directors to be constantly on the alert. All the same it should not be forgotten that certain psychological components of a more or less pathological nature do not necessarily prevent spiritual development. The practice of the Church attests this. In a canonization cause, for example, the heroism of virtue is confirmed without, however, any willingness to make a pronouncement on the character—supernatural, natural or morbid—of para-mystical or simply abnormal phenomena. Where a realistic mind and a virtuous will go together, it is possible and sometimes necessary to ignore certain psychic features which would otherwise constitute a serious impediment. All the more reason for trying to reach an objective and impartial judgment of the required aptitudes as a whole.

5. THE COMBINED JUDGMENT PASSED BY THE AUTHORITIES

We have several times urged the calling in of specialists for problems requiring their skill. Their intervention is necessary in order to cut short all hesitation and to give a firm basis for the superiors' judgment. But it is the superiors who have to make the final synthesis; they alone can pass judgment about a candidate's suitability.

The positive judgment concerning the suitability of a particular candidate is written into a rule of life of which the superiors with the Church's official mandate are the guarantors and custodians.

Thus it is for them to decide whether a candidate is really suitable for the type of life of which they are the representatives. This final judgment, while based on the contribution of the specialists and collaborators, is not scientific in the strict sense of the word. It embraces so many imponderables that it demands far more a clear-sighted view of the whole case than an analysis of component parts.

A prudent judgment of this sort subsumes all the viewpoints described above and may be summed up in a single question. This could be the one asked by Cardinal Verdier when admitting the priests of his diocese to orders: 'Will he be happy? Will he make others happy?' In its concise simplicity and its far-reaching significance these phrases unify wonderfully all the elements that have just been so laboriously analysed.

The physical, psychological and spiritual aptitudes of candidates have been the object of this inquiry. The reader will have noticed for himself that they are mainly connected with the detection of negative symptoms and indications against a vocation, with a view to taking them into account or to providing an effective remedy. There are good reasons for this negative procedure. It is, in fact, the only one possible. The desired qualities are so varied that it would be irksome to draw up an inventory of them, and far from easy to verify them. And there would be no justification for it. Since a divine vocation is, in fact, a gracious invitation from the Lord, it would scarcely seem possible to reduce it to a collection of dispositions or gifts, however brilliant it might be. So long as the minimum aptitudes are present there is the possibility of a vocation. To find out how the response is to be made and on what criteria, it is necessary to go on from the discernment of aptitudes (or external vocation) to that of the personal call (or internal vocation).

CHAPTER IV

THE DISCERNMENT OF INTERNAL VOCATION

A CANDIDATE's aptitude to the priestly or religious life is to be sought at various levels of his personality; at every level, it can be assessed by experiential data systematized into a coherent whole with its own proper laws. But can the same be said of internal grace, which, like all supernatural facts, surely eludes direct observation and exact verification?

1. THE CRITERIA PROVIDED BY THE CHURCH'S EXPERIENCE

Of course, we cannot detect the presence of grace nor submit it to outside control. But does this mean we cannot observe or verify it in any way at all? Grace, being a supernatural force received by man, produces its own effects. Its operation affects the whole man, even to his conscience. One person asks himself whether he has a vocation; a second desires to respond to it; a third decides to commit himself. But we cannot ignore the fact that these questions, desires and decisions might arise from other, purely human sources. This makes circumspection necessary. Not everything which is good in itself is necessarily the good which this particular person ought to do in given circumstances. We must enquire from what source (or what spirit, as spiritual writers commonly put it) the idea of vocation has come in each individual case. How can we choose what norms are to be laid down, what criteria followed, to achieve this end?

Here the Church's experience as a spiritual community under the guidance of the Holy Spirit proves of great assistance. From among the spiritual experiences of all ages, it has admitted a handful as authentic: by ratifying the work of the founders of orders and congregations, the Church certifies that their spirit comes from God and leads back to him. Anyone who finds the same spirit in himself can with good reason consider himself called to the same way of life. By setting the candidate in that current, begun by the Holy Spirit himself through the privileged experience of the founder, we can confirm whether or not he shares in the same corporate grace. This is surely the real point of the period of 'probation' or 'trial' which centuries' old practice has required of every candidate to the religious life.

But even before he commits himself to this initial period (which is valid only in so far as it is seen as preliminary to a definitive commitment it is wise to find out whether the candidate is right to make the attempt: to this end, we must find out whether he is moved by the same spirit, towards the same end. So the examination is in two stages, and may end by demonstrating the presence of an internal vocation in the soul. The first enquiry limits itself to whether the grounds for his desire are authentic: the verification of motive. The second considers whether his desire bears authentic fruit in its effects: verification of spiritual results.

Hitherto, we have considered only the call to religious life. Since the different forms of religious life have been set down in the rules and constitutions, and recognized at one particular moment of history and through a specific intervention of the hierarchical authorities, it becomes relatively easy to determine and verify the particular spirit of each religious family.

The life of a secular priest is not so clearly defined because it has not been so closely specified. But it, too, has been ratified. In the course of centuries, authorized directives have been issued, to define in greater detail that which had been sparked off by sacerdotal graces.

Just as the rules codify the privileged experience of the founders, so these directives ratify the experience of the Church. In both cases the hierarchical authority stands guarantor of the authentic character of the spiritual experiences and aspirations, of the forms of life adopted and the apostolic methods in general use.

In all cases of presumed vocation precise points for guidance and properly established criteria do exist. The priest consulted must know these and understand them. Simply to have read about them and to have a theoretical understanding of them is not sufficient. One must have first-hand experience of spiritual facts before they will reveal their secret. In order to say whether the spirit of a vocation is genuine the priest needs not only a thorough knowledge of the candidate but must also be entirely familiar with the particular spirituality the candidate wishes to adopt. The persons best placed for this are those who live by the same spirit: directors and superiors. This brings us back once more to the real point of the period of probation and formation, both for the candidate and for those responsible for discerning his vocation. The former must learn awareness of the spirit which supports him by comparing it with that of the group into which he has launched himself. The latter also must take note of his conformity or divergence, as the case may be.

Seen from this angle, the ways of grace which at first sight seem disconcerting take on their full meaning. Benedict Labre, Don Bosco, Charles de Foucauld after many years quit the spiritual family to which they belonged, because daily confrontation taught them that their calling lay elsewhere. Were they mistaken in entering? That is not the right way of looking at the question. They needed a valid confrontation in order to discover their own individual calling, the character of which eluded them. Nor can it be said that they disclaimed their past by leaving. Rather, their past grew into a future, which was not better in itself but which realized better the call of God which sounded in their souls. Benedict Labre, Don Basco and Charles de Foucauld did not claim that to be a wretched beggar, a Salesian or a hermit in Tamanrasset was better than to be a monk, a secular priest or a Cistercian. What they asserted, what they made the substance of their lives, was that it is necessary to follow the Spirit of God, not to dictate to it.

We find the same outlook in the truly spiritual descriptions of all who become aware of the authenticity of the divine call. Two instances out of thousands come to mind: St Ignatius Loyola, gradually discovering from personal experience the way of life he was to set before his 'sons'; and Newman, discovering in the same way the meaning of his membership of the Oratory of his 'father', St Philip Neri. Theologians, masters of spirituality and shrewd biographers all vouch for the testimony of these two. We reproduce two texts, separated by some four hundred years, so that the reader may judge the identical spirit that informs them.

Jerome Nadal, one of St Ignatius' first disciples and in the founder's closest confidence, recorded more than the wonderful legends of a prophetic vision, in which the blue-print of the Society was revealed to the future superior general. This is how he describes the work of providence in the Saint's soul: 'From the time Ignatius was in Paris, he did not pursue only his studies. He was equally studious to know where the spirit and the call of God were leading him. This end was none other than the foundation of a religious order. Yet, with great personal modesty he followed the spirit which led him, and took care not to run ahead of it. In this manner he was led towards a goal he did not himself perceive, and made his way thither with a wise improvidence, with the simplicity of a heart deep-rooted in Christ ... At Rome, Ignatius began to conceive in more detail the founding of an order; since he had left this world he had been directed to this goal, gently, step by step, by the Spirit of God.'★

Father Louis Bouyer sums up in a few spiritually concise lines of the whole development of Newman's vocation as an Oratorian: 'The Oratory, which to begin with he had taken up as a result of the elimination of other plans, rather than because it presented any positive attraction in itself, had now become very dear to him. Following its rule, it is himself that he finds again, as Catholic and priest, in St Philip's ideal, and ever more and more, as that ideal becomes the very texture of his own existence. Slowly and surely, without his knowing it or consciously willing it, the form and figure of the Saint who created the Oratory grows clearer —to his eyes shall we say? or to his inward vision? Philip, for him, is now ... as though he were his second self. He reveals to him possibilities, till then hidden within the depths of his being,

---

★ Both texts are taken from Jerome Nadal's *Dialogi de Societate,* published in the *Fontes Narrativi Societatis Jesu,* vol. II, Rome, pp. 252 and 259. Since the original Latin texts are so compact, they will be given here: 'Quo tempore Lutetiae fuit, non solum studia litterarum sectatus est, sed animum simul intendit quo spiritus illum ac divina vocatio ducebat, ad Ordinem religiosum instituendum; tametsi singulari animi modestia ducentem spiritum sequebatur, non praeibat. Itaque deducebatur quo nesciebat suaviter, nec enim de Ordinis institutione tunc cogitabat; et tamen pedetentim ad illum et viam muniebat et iter faciebat, quasi sapienter imprudens, in simplicitate cordis sui in Christo.'— '(Romae) Propius vero iam spectare coepit Ignatius ad ordinem instituendum, quo iam inde ab initio sui secessus suaviter ac pedetentim a spiritu Dei dirigebatur.' Nadal continues: 'Tota ratio instituti fere sumpta est ex actis Ignatii atque instituto vitae, quod habuit inde postquam a Deo vocatus est, donec Ordinem instituerit; ut prius intelligatur Deum in ipso institutum quasi primis lineis delineasse, et si velis, exemplar constituisse, ex quo formaretur Societas.' (*ibid.*).

and illumines his everyday countenance with a calm and tranquil light, in striking contrast with the shadows that encompass him.'★

Eventual, full, positive discernment, which begins from the entry into a way of life, is the outcome of a slow process of maturing. Essentially it must be made by the person himself. Spiritual directors and superiors are its privileged witnesses; the most they can do is to help it along indirectly by stressing the merits of the case for a vocation. The rôle of the consultant priest is generally more restricted. The question he has to answer is whether or not there is room for supposing a call from God. All priests should be able to give some answer, at least provisionally.

It is hoped that we have gone into sufficient detail about what constitutes definite discernment of the particular type of life to be chosen and how the answer may be put to the test. In the rest of this chapter, our attention will be focused on the question of how it can be verified that there is a divine call to the priestly or religious life.

2. SINCERITY AND RIGHTNESS OF INTENTION

It lies with the priest who is consulted about the spiritual validity of a presumed vocation to verify it. He must be impartial, for any verification supposes an objective comparison of the facts under examination with regularly established norms. For such a comparison to be objective, and therefore valid, the priest must know how to get at the facts in each individual case and must possess criteria to which he can refer. Perception on both the spiritual and the human levels is indispensable if he is to carry out his task conscientiously.

★ Louis BOUYER, *Newman, His Life and Spirituality,* London, 1958, p. 342.

To get at the individual facts in a particular case, insight into human affairs will be an invaluable help. It will be reinforced by sticking to a few elementary but very profitable rules.

Since what we are looking for are personal, concrete facts, above all about his inner life, the candidate himself must provide them. It would certainly be wrong to show oneself unduly suspicious, and so cast doubt on the sincerity of the candidate. Any intentional deception will show up in the evasions which such deception necessitates. But a more subtle danger lies in wait, for the priest as much as for the candidate himself. Both may be taken in by a sincerity that misleads. Certainly, sincerity does exclude deliberate lying and deception; but it can also lead to candid statements made in real (and therefore not culpable) ignorance of what lies deep down. Sincerity does not necessarily go hand in hand with correct judgment or, as spiritual authors say, rightness of intention.

The priest consulted must make up for such gaps, and he has every chance of succeeding if he acts without any bias in the matter at all. He should make it possible for the candidate to express himself with complete freedom and without any constraint. There should be no cut-and-dried formula for conducting the interview, and no preliminary outline of the criteria or norms to which the candidate has to adapt himself. The candidate should be left to reveal at leisure his feelings and opinions, his desires and aspirations, his achievements and setbacks. It is for the candidate to put forward what seems to him important and to emphasize his shortcomings.

His account of himself may remain incomplete: he may lose sight of certain aspects or pass over others in silence. Help will then be given, but without influencing him in any way. The questions asked should be neutral, or they may cause a reaction in one direction or the other by the phrasing or meaningful tone used in presenting them.

Any direct interrogation is liable to distort the answers. If a set of questions has to be asked they should be formulated as alternatives whose terms are effectively equivalent. It is useless to ask: 'Is your prayer personal?—Have you a true desire to serve God? —You are not selfish?' It is better to ask: 'Is your prayer personal or communal?—Have you a true desire to serve God whether as layman or as priest?—Do you feel that your own interests occupy you too much or not enough?'

The second sort of questions do not, as the first, elicit monosyllabic replies (yes, no) or laconic ones (of course, certainly, probably, perhaps, I don't think so, etc.), which by their very brevity give no real information at all. On the contrary they lead to a more delicate, thorough and accurate appraisal of the candidate's personal dispositions. They keep the conversation going without any disconcerting breaks.

This is described in technical language as an *entretien nondirectif*. It means that the consultant priest deliberately refrains from steering the candidate in one direction or another by his attitudes, judgments, insinuations or questions. The one result, to be obtained at all costs, is to give him every possible opportunity to express himself as he is. In this way the interviewer himself can become aware of what animates him deep down.★

As one becomes familiar with such a procedure (and to acquire it needs flexibility, practice and perseverance), one can make out without too much difficulty explanations which are theoretical, bor-

---

★ The few details given do not exhaust the subject of interview technique. It is hoped that in a further volume we will have more to say about this. Prudently applied, it makes for smoother contacts between directors and their charges, and facilitates the verification of motivations and spiritual results. On this point it will be profitable to consult the articles by Fr. A. Godin, S.J., published in the *Nouvelle Revue Théologique,* particularly: *Les fonctions psychologiques dans la relation pastorale,* 1958, pp. 606-14; *L'accueil dans le dialogue pastoral,* 1958, pp. 934-43 and *Le transfert dans la relation pastorale,* 1959, pp. 400-12 and 824-35, and 1960, pp. 141-57.

rowed from writers or current usuage and put forward in good faith, or accounts which do express an interior experience, however lifeless the terminology employed may be.

Then the spiritual insight of the priest must come into play. Knowledge of the ways of grace, personally experienced and at the same time objectively analysed, will give him his bearings and the criteria he needs.

Would it be asking too much to expect every priest to have reflected seriously on his own spiritual progress? and even to expect him to have compared it with experiences which the church has recognized as authentic? For if he is to guide others well, he must beware of thinking of everything in terms of a single, strictly personal experience, however valid this may be. In our Father's house there are many mansions and many ways leading to them.

The diversity of vocations, as well as their fundamental convergence, can only be recognized after assiduous spiritual reflection. This is what gives such enormous interest to a thorough study of the vocations of the saints, at least when we do not confine ourselves to miraculous elements which are often quite exterior to the truly spiritual, but look for grace and its mysterious ways. We have not drawn this distinction between human and spiritual insight, in order to separate them or set them in opposition to each other. In practice they are one, and complement one another all the time in the person of the priest who is consulted.

3. THE VERIFICATION OF MOTIVES

Now that we have described the nature of the required verification and of its procedure, the time has come to say something about its actual working. We have already shown that grace, incomprehensible in itself, affects the conscious mind both in the aspirations it excites and in the fruits it bears. When a candidate offers himself, the spiritual fruits are at most a promise of future flowering. The first thing to examine will be the authenticity of his aspirations, and this is where the examination of motives comes in.

The examination of motives is basically the verification of a single constant factor. In all ages the Church has held that only the total love and exclusive service of God are the basis of a vocation. Since the second commandment does not differ from the first, it need not be said that the determination to give oneself entirely to God goes hand in hand with a charity towards one's neighbour. Depending on individual cases, personal consecration assumes the forms called contemplative or active. Contemplation or union with God and activity or the shining forth of this love must never be thought of as mutually exclusive. Neither goes without the other. Total love of God and of one's neighbour in God is the essence of any vocation.

This love, like any working of grace, is embedded in the very conditions of our human existence. It is futile to try and discover it in the pure state: this would be to dessicate it, to disincarnate it. The way we envisage it, the inspiration we draw from it, the resolution it fires us with, the effects it produces—all its repercussions take concrete forms. One person will desire to leave the world, another will decide to devote himself to caring for orphans, yet another will seek a life of austerity and privation.

All these forms—and they are legion—may be the expression of a supernatural impulse; but this is not always the case. Some people flee the world in pursuit of a painful illusion, others take an interest in abandoned children as a protest against what they consider to be flagrant injustices, others again seek refuge in misery and abjection from some unconscious resentment. The verification of motives is therefore concerned with the reasons actually put forward by the candidate; it aims to find out whether or not his motives really do spring from a deep love of God.

And, in fact, we will always find motives which are human. There is no need to be afraid of this; it would be absurd to declare outright that since the motives are human the call is inauthentic. A patient examination of the significance and the tendencies of motives is required. Three sorts of motivation appear. First, those bearing immediately on personal advantages; second, those which, although of a spiritual nature, betray misunderstanding or ignorance of their real meaning; and third, all those which express, in their own way and of course very imperfectly, a fundamental desire to give all to God. We will now consider these three types, so that the characteristics of each will be more apparent.

Insufficient motives

In this first category come motives which seek personal advantage. They need not be confined to purely material considerations: income, personal welfare, life without financial worries, etc. They may be of a more elevated nature: emotional support, personal fulfilment, intellectual standing, etc.

They are not necessarily bad in themselves. Every man has the right and the duty to secure a reasonable standard of living for himself; the desire to further one's education or to make a career are worthy. But anyone who seeks to use the priestly or religious state as a means of self-advancement is grossly deceiving himself. Instead of engaging himself in the Lord's service, he engages the Lord to serve him. This turns everything upside down. Seen in cold print, such a reversal of values seems quite ridiculous, almost monstrous.

For this reason many priests are inclined to dismiss it out of hand. They are unwilling to believe that candidates could be capable of such cynical calculation or such flagrant duplicity. Experience, however, confirms that this reversal of values is quite common. But we must add at once that it is almost always the result of false reasoning, carried out in good faith. This should not be forgotten if we are to come to the aid of those who are victims of it.

Candidates driven by the motive of temporal self-interest do in fact justify their decision by rationalizations like this: 'What finer or better thing is there than the life of a priest or religious? If at the same time it has the advantages I seek, then I shall be killing two birds with one stone!' They are generally well pleased with their discovery, in which the abstract value of the supernatural conceals the self-centredness of their decision. They defend their vocation by deceiving themselves about their true motive. Not for several years do they become aware of the ambiguity of their choice. Often they find that their state does not carry the anticipated advantages; and in any case they have a vague feeling that however enviable this state may be, it only shows its bright side to those who give themselves to it entirely, without any ulterior motives.

We may tumble across such motives before entry, when the candidate is fired with enthusiasm for his idea. We may also discover them much later, when he is bitterly disillusioned at finding only wretchedness and vexation in the ashes of his hopes.

In both cases it is important to try and understand these victims of illusion in order to be able to help them. In revealing the futility of their motives, do not handle them roughly, nor reproachfully. They will inevitably take umbrage. Their good faith was real and so they cannot, without unfairness, be accused of culpable deceit or base calculation. Their good faith was simply caught unawares, and they should be helped to realize the motives they acted upon: particularly since these motives are not usually bad in themselves. The real meaning of the priesthood and the religious life should be carefully explained to them. As a rule they are very willing to take stock of themselves and even to recognize their mistake and rectify their decision.

A young religious who had gone into the noviciate because he was afraid of the responsibilities of life, summed up the conversation in which he had at last clearly seen the insufficiency of his motives in these words: 'All that remains is to go myself and ask to leave, and show I am not the coward I thought I was!'

A few examples will let these motives be better seen.

John was the eldest in a family of ten children. An exemplary choirboy and first in his class at the village school, he was enabled to go on with his classical studies thanks to the intervention of the parish priest. He loved his studies. If he entered the seminary or the noviciate his parents would willingly accept the sacrifice this vocation would mean for the family; but if he did not continue towards the priesthood they would take it for granted that he should come to help on the farm, once his secondary schooling was over. John resolutely settled for the noviciate. From philosopy onwards an indefinable uneasiness took hold of him, which seemed the more inexplicable since he had no complaints about anyone or anything, and everyone was very pleased with him. It was only after three years of uncertainty that he realized his true motive: the studies interested him enormously, but not the religious life.

Charles was the son of well-off parents. His father, a forceful man, wanted his sons to learn life the hard way, and so he made no contribution towards their upkeep at university—it was for them to find the money. The two eldest ones managed very well: one obtained a grant and the other found lucrative employment during the vacations. Charles felt unable to do all this. No profession attracted him: they all presented him with tasks beyond his powers. During his second term in the sixth form he was still undecided about what to do. He complained to a fellow pupil, who replied jokingly: 'I thought you were going to become a monk!' All of a sudden a gleam of hope showed on the horizon. Charles went into a monastery, which made it unnecessary to choose a career and fend for himself. Gradually dissatisfaction crept over him. At the end of four years he confessed, not without regret at seeing that his only escape was also apparently closed to him: 'What else could I do?'

Louis was twenty-four, not very gifted and seemingly unsuited to the responsibilities of the apostolate. He held on desperately to his vows and the prospect of becoming a priest. He kept on piling up all sorts of reasons for continuing in his vocation, but behind them all lay the thought: 'I was a great baby, and I wanted to grow up. A priest must be a real man, and so I made up my mind to become a priest at all costs, so that I could turn into a man.'

These are three very sketchy cases, but they do illustrate the point. They are not at all uncommon, and the Church's directives regularly refer to them.★ His Holiness Pope Pius XII not long ago recommended careful attention to them. Seminarists, he said, should not be tempted to 'remain in a life which is not suited to them, reasoning like the unfaithful steward: "To dig I am unable; to beg I am ashamed!"'

It must not be thought that the presence of apparently spiritual

---

★ Ecclesiastical documents do not hesitate to set out in detail the great variety of individual motives which are wrongly used to justify entry into the seminary or religious life. The encyclical *Ad Catholici Sacerdotii* lists a few of them; the instructions *Quam Ingens* and *Magna Equidem* are even more explicit. Among others they indicate: the desire to have an easy life, to obtain honorific appointments, to escape manual work, to be exempted from military service, etc., in short, to use the priesthood or the religious state in order to attain to a higher or easier level of life. Other motives are also considered: the fear of losing one's soul or going to hell if one returns to the world. Finally they also emphasize that these motives are often concealed, even without the knowledge of those who are victims to them or nourish them, beneath nobler appearances or more elevated motives, which are invoked without any real basis in the behaviour of the person himself.

motives excludes the possibility of such obviously insufficient motivation. Whether by simulating, rationalizing, or deference to public opinion candidates deck out the advantages they seek in a pseudo-religious garb. There are innumerable variations on the themes, but a few salient features can be indicated. Some appeal to the supposed certainty of salvation for those who go into religion or become priests. Others are looking for a community which will shore up their vacillating will-power, an obedience which makes any personal initiative superfluous, or a sheltering wall against their fear of the realities of life (social, sexual, marital, etc.) which removes the need to face up to them. And others again want to allay their torturing anxiety by choosing the most perfect life there is.

All these motives lean on spiritual and religious values with the one aim of compensating for sometimes considerable personal deficiencies. In all the attitudes described there lurks a strongly marked self-centredness. The candidate is looking for tranquillity, protection, relief. The fact that for this purpose he turns to spiritual considerations or religious institutions makes no difference to his fundamentally self-centred inspiration.

Here again, candidates are not committing themselves to a life in and with God; what they are trying to do is engage God in their own lives. Without knowing or realizing it, they are letting themselves be guilty of the same complete reversal of values. But because they think they are attaching themselves to the spiritual, they learn all the quicker how futile their efforts are, while at the same time clinging ever more desperately to them. The strain soon becomes unbearable, and so it is important for the priest to whom they turn to locate the sore spot at once, so that it does not fester.

The priest, called on to bring such motivation into the open, finds himself faced with a very delicate task. He must beware of condemning the candidate and yet avoid confirming him in his resolution. With tact, moderation and patience he should help the candidate to disentangle his motives and show him the mistaken idea he has formed of spiritual values and truths. Sometimes he will fail, because considerable psychic factors are at work. He will then have to use his authority to point the error out clearly and command him, if need be, to take up the matter with his superiors.

This sort of motivation is found particularly in those who complain that they are getting nothing, or not enough, out of religious life or the seminary, that the formation is worthless or that the tasks assigned them are too heavy: in short, that they are being asked to waste their energies for nothing, to expose themselves to risks and to work themselves to the bone. They expect everything to be handed to them on a plate, other people to put themselves out for them, and all risks and difficulties to be removed from their path. The very fact of having entered the seminary or noviciate appears to them as the perfect sacrifice, and once this sacrifice has been made they expect their hundred-fold. They complain of the order of the day, the practices of prayer, the whole way of life. They demand greater poverty, a more expansive and universal charity, and stricter observance. Their complaints and demands are usually directed at other people. They are so preoccupied with all this that they completely forget to consider and examine their own personal commitment.

Inadequate motives

The second type of motive is quite distinct from the first. It is concerned with the presence of motives which are religious and in themselves valid, but are marred by one lack: they are invoked wrongly because they do not correspond to the end for which they were put forward. The proper word for them is 'inadequate'. A few examples will show how it is possible to be at once religious and yet unsuitable.

Henry was a seminarist satisfactory from every point of view.

His director may have been obliged to moderate certain excesses in bodily mortifications, but his untiring charity and persistence in prayer seemed to be sure signs of a true vocation. A year before ordination his father died of a sudden stroke. Henry was violently shaken by the news and came back completely dazed from the funeral. As he did not get over the shock and seemed deeply disturbed, he was sent away for a rest. He returned to the seminary worse than ever. Finally he told his spiritual director the real cause of his interior struggle. When, at the age of twelve, he had learnt that his father had rejected his faith, Henry had vowed to become a priest in order to obtain his conversion by this sacrifice. The sudden death of his father meant that no priest could have assisted him. And after the funeral his father's will disclosed a profession of atheism. As a result Henry could no longer see any meaning in his becoming a priest and could do nothing but accuse God.

Madeleine, the daughter of a worthy and respected family, was an exemplary novice. Her novice-mistress, a sensible woman, could reproach her for only one fault: her prudery. Shortly after her first vows, Madeleine grew melancholy without any apparent reason, becoming more and more reserved and sullen, to the great surprise of her community and superiors. Urged to open herself entirely to a spiritual director, she admitted that her brother, four years older than herself, had led her into sexual practices when she was only thirteen. For two years she had frequently consented to his indecent proposals. At fifteen, during a retreat, she was stricken with remorse and confessed to the retreat-giver who gave her absolution, but not without stressing very vigorously the seriousness of incest. Under the force of his words Madeleine tried to suppress even the memory of what had happened, but without success. Frightened by the persistence of these memories, Madeleine decided to expiate her sins by forbidding herself the joys of marriage and motherhood. In the noviciate everything went very well, but shortly after her vows she received a visit from one of her sisters who came to show her her first baby. All of a sudden Madeleine felt shattered by the sight of the little creature. She tried to repress her disturbance but remained torn between the longing for motherhood she was stifling as a temptation and the fear of being unfaithful to the sacrifice she had laid on herself.

It can easily be seen that the crises which—fortunately, one might say—came into the open in both these cases are due to the candidate's failure to realize the true meaning of engaging himself in orders or religious life. It is as clear as daylight that a serious error of perspective has crept into their reasoning.

The life of a priest or religious—just like any other Christian life—necessarily involves sacrifices, either as propitiation or as expiation. No one doubts this. But to reduce the priesthood merely to expiation is to ignore its sacramental meaning and its very essence. To make religious life simply a penance is just as mistaken. A crisis will inevitably crop up sooner or later, when the candidate realizes that the means he thought absolutely efficacious are not so, and for good reason; or when he perceives, vaguely and without knowing fully how or why, that his whole life is out of line. When ideas like this are reduced to their main outlines, the mistaken perspective becomes glaringly obvious; its victims, however, scarcely realize that they are distorting the truth.

There is no reason to be amazed at such naivety or blindness. The mental confusion which follows a sharp awakening to reality may be fatal if it is not accepted with clearness and understanding. One must beware of giving any more shocks to those who feel what they had thought to be the solid ground of their vocation suddenly slipping away from under their feet. There is no bad will in them. It has very often been clumsy exhortations or misunderstood recommendations which have distorted their vision.

In all kindness, the spiritual validity of their avowed motives should be accurately appraised, and their subjective aspirations compared with the objective demands of any vocation worthy of the name. Then they usually feel able to reconsider their decision with full knowledge. Either they will feel liberated because the net in which they were caught has now been torn open, and rediscover their happiness by leaving a way of life which they were unsuited to; or they will feel a new lease of life because the structures they have mistakenly tried to erect have all been swept away, and find peace of soul by setting themselves in a genuinely religious way on a path whose real direction escaped them in their confusion.

Inadequate motivation is nothing like as frequent as insufficient motivation, yet it should not be ignored. It is more liable to put people on the wrong scent because it urges them towards enthusiasm and zeal. Misplaced enthusiasm and exaggerated zeal, perhaps, but often forceful enough to carry candidates on even after their final commitment. If the crisis comes to a head only then, it is very much more difficult to put it right.

Valid motives

The third type of motive is not essentially distinct from those we have been examining. Externally they may even seem to be identical. But as a class they have one characteristic in common: all possess an inner core of truth. Behind them lies a total and exclusive love which is inspired by God and leads directly to him. The desire to study, to become holy, to help those cut off from God, to find silence and recollection, to leave the turmoil of the world behind, to fly from frivolity and pleasure, and so on, is in this instance sustained and carried forward by a will which directs the whole being towards God. The spiritual inexperience of the candidate makes him more liable to stress the actual overflowing of divine grace which is immediately felt, rather than the spiritual impetus itself.

Such a way of expressing themselves, translating everything into human terms, is hardly surprising in young men or women, who very rarely have an adequate vocabulary even when their experience of grace is real. The years of formation exist to help them purify their intentions and express themselves more accurately. The internal vocation only gradually reaches its full vigour as a spiritual driving-force as part of a spiritual growth which—it is to be hoped—will be continued to the end of their lives.

A missionary vocation will have to get rid of the romantic elements which are so often a marked feature at the beginning. An active vocation will have to fathom the true meaning of apostolic activity so as to avoid confusing it with feverish and self-defeating activism. A contemplative vocation will have to discover the positive spiritual content of interior recollection or else founder in emptiness resulting from the absence of any external preoccupation. Only the slow process of exploring all the spiritual dimensions implicit in the initial motives can give sustenance, nourishment and value to the life of a priest or religious at the level of personal maturity.

The motives on which the decision appeared to be based at the beginning are usually purified gradually—most candidates only realize this afterwards. Indeed, this realization is made much more during the actual process of growth than through any explicit reflection. Thus it is quite normal for a young man to attribute his vocation to a priest whose spirituality he admires, and in the same way many a girl can trace her vocation back to fortuitous contacts with nuns whose simplicity, charity and recollection she appreciated. There is nothing to worry about there. These young people have discovered spiritual values, embodied in a person or group, which stirs a response in themselves. Vividly impressed with what they see in others, they become aware of the desire to do the same, or at least feel it might be possible. Many saints have acted this way, rushing along the path of renunciation with the motto: 'Quod isti et illi, cur non ego?'—'If others have done it, why shouldn't I, too?'

It goes without saying that mere imitation of the external actions and attitudes of these models must gradually give way to a discovery of that element in themselves which responded in the first place. Unless this happens there will never be any understanding of the personal vocation which, although forming part of a community setting and having much in common with other people, will always remain an individual matter.

As the purifying of these valid motives progresses, the inner gift shines more and more brightly through the initial impulses and imperceptibly transfigures them. Sometimes, however, this maturing process is held in check: the initial impulses so preoccupy the candidate's mind that they obstruct development. Then all of a sudden they appear so hollow and unfounded that a more or less dramatic crisis ensues, as is shown in the following two cases.

Sister Caroline entered religious life at eighteen. In the noviciate her fervent yet amenable nature, her cheerful readiness to help others and her whole religious attitude made a favourable impression. The Mother General let her go on for six years of further formation, and immediately after her profession entrusted her with very important tasks. Sister Caroline carried these out to the satisfaction of all. Five years later, aged thirty-two, she asked the superior general whether she really was satisfactory. The superior, a little surprised at this question, tried to put her mind at rest and said again that she was sure of her suitability and her vocation. Noticing, however, that her words had no effect, she advised her to discuss her problem thoroughly with her spiritual director.

Sister Caroline followed this advice. She told her director that she had never thought about religious life until she was seventeen. Certainly she had very great esteem for the nuns among whom she had been brought up, but the only ideal she thought of for a woman was making a home and raising a family. She was passionately fond of children. The last year at school turned her outlook on the future upside down. Her form-mistress was a newly arrrived sister for whom she conceived limitless admiration. During the second term she decided to take the religious habit: she, too, wanted to put all the gifts she had received at the Lord's disposal. During her years of formation she had overcome all her difficulties by remembering the high stature, the vivid words and the enthusiasm of her 'model'. Great was her dismay when she had learnt, a few months before, that this exemplary religious had left the convent. The mystery surrounding this unexpected departure tormented and paralysed her. She felt she had lost her grip and she could find no support anywhere. At first she was seized by bitter disillusionment, as though some personal wrong had been done to her. She then became aware that she was bearing a constant grudge. She had the impression that she had been deceived, that she might have been the victim of illusion when she entered religion. Her religious life, which she had thought to be fervent, seemed only a pose. Never, she said, had she really prayed: she had merely gone through the motions and no more. She had never given herself to others, but had simply tried to find herself in an offering which she was the first to admire!

When she had laid all these reflections before her director, she thought she should make known one other factor. Something in the depths of her being—where and how, she could not even start to say—was urging her to make a resolution. Since she wanted to give herself entirely to God, she would apply herself faithfully to prayer, devote herself to her work and never refuse even the slightest service to others. She asked her director to let her live for a month in this spirit to find out what God intended for her. When the month was over she had an experience which surprised her at first, but then gave her new strength. Without any attempt on her part she had been several times drawn to prayer, even in the midst of her work. As she said, it was not a matter of going down on her knees, but of continuing with her work *coram Domino*. On each occasion she had noticed a sort of certainty and serenity which filled her whole being and transfigured her occupations. The conclusion she came to was quite simple: hitherto she had tried to keep her religious life going by fastening it to external postures, but now she proposed to anchor it in God. She then understood that the sudden loss of her 'model', to whom she had conformed herself in everything, had made this deeper insight possible. She summed up her whole past experience in a striking sentence: 'Until now I have been living by an idea I had formed of the spiritual life; but now God has favoured me with a spiritual experience I can really live by.'

At seventeen, Peter had been admitted to the postulancy of a congregation of teaching brothers. Pleasant, lively, intelligent and impulsive he won his novice-master's sympathy from the start. His alert and lively mind was not as naive as people liked to think. Peter soon realized that he could take advantage of it to get what he wanted from his superiors. He was allowed to study at university, where he brought off fairly considerable successes, which made him feel very pleased. Yet as the last year at university went on and the date of his perpetual vows came nearer, a persistent uneasiness took hold of him.

He went to see a priest and told him that this anxiety came from a definite cause. For some years he had not been at all careful about this vow of poverty. He was spending quite a large amount on his small pleasures, money which had been made over to him by the congregation for legitimate expenses. He had gradually been making more generous estimates of his expenses for study purposes. The fact that he was living in a strange house had made such manipulations easier. Several times, though, he had decided to put a stop to these practices; but to his consternation he invariably found himself being carried on by habit, and he feared this might become second nature.

A few conversations with the priest he consulted let him take a hold on himself. But the improvement itself, by freeing his attention, made it evident to him that the whole of his religious attitude was at fault. His breaches of poverty were the consequence rather than the cause of his uneasiness. He had to make a choice: either he would spend the whole of his life following his personal interests, or he would give first place to God. All this made him reflect on the motives which had led him to enter religion. While still quite young, he was convinced that the religious life was heaven on earth, and he thought of all his fellow religious as saints. It was sufficient to join the community to become a saint and to get to heaven 'without any trouble'. Before he had even started to embezzle any money, he had been 'embezzling' religious life. And so he wondered whether he ought not to make a complete break and live as a layman. Nevertheless he still had a very real desire to serve God. He gave himself to prayer, tried hard to be helpful to others, gained more detachment and obeyed his superiors rather than twisting them round his finger. After a few months he realized that he was starting to discover the real meaning of religious life. His past defects, which he had thought to be insurmountable because he could never forgive himself for them, were actually helping him to acquire humility. At last he had discovered the cause of what had been wrong. Until then he had been attempting to manage everything by himself and for himself. Thenceforth he would respond to the urgings of grace without overrating himself. At his final vows, his original decision, though deficient, was made into something better by his sincere and wholehearted offering.

In these two cases, as in many others of the same sort, the real purpose of the divine impulse is only slowly recognized. Such an imperfect understanding of the action of grace, however real it may be, can easily be explained. Grace takes hold of a man as he is: if his attitude is immature, his response to grace will be affected more or less profoundly by this immaturity. This is why the verification of any particular motivation will always be a delicate undertaking. The question is one of determining whether grace is really at work, even when it is superficially deformed by personal dispositions, or whether the personal dispositions are leading to desires and decisions which are not the result of an invitation of grace. In the latter event there is deficient motivation; in the former there is a valid motivation which needs purifying.

It is necessary to have a clear idea of the significance of these three types of motivation. Motivations differ from one another and receive their distinctive character by the relation between the motives brought forward and the ends to which they are applied, and not so much by the motives in themselves. This relation can be deprived of all objective foundation (first type: insufficient motivation); or inadequately founded (second type: inadequate motivation); or validly founded (third type: valid motivation). But since perfection is not of this world, even valid motivation can be expressed in none too happy ways, or made up of impure elements, or hindered by self-centredness and even plain selfishness.

There is never any need to dwell too long on motives alone, for they do not by themselves settle once and for all the question of discerning an internal vocation. The point to concentrate on is the verification of the motivation as such. If this is authentic, even though it may still be in an embryonic stage, it will allow disparate elements which are impure or too human to be gradually removed, if they are caught in time and treated without undue haste. It should not be forgotten that any call from God makes itself heard in a human being and is perceived in a human way, with all the mental and spiritual accompaniments of the human person. Surely the whole meaning of the priestly or religious life is to bring the candidate to understand our Lord more fully by living in him and by him.

It may happen, however, that the priest consulted remains doubtful. Certain motivations cannot be fathomed or simply elude any systematic examination, while others remain suspect in spite of apparently authentic features. In such cases he often asks himself: 'Would it be wise to attach greater importance to the negative elements in order to avoid prolonging an inauthentic commitment? Or would it be better to leave grace all possible chance to work?' This is surely not a real dilemma: temporizing never gives grace more chance to work; yet no final decision should be made while doubt is still present. To remove any lingering hesitations it should be remembered that another criterion is available: whether the candidate's attitude bears any spiritual results.

4. THE VERIFICATION OF SPIRITUAL RESULTS

To verify the effects of grace when a candidate has not yet spent many years in the life he has embraced is not as easy as some people like to think. It is not a matter of establishing whether or not a candidate is generous, faithful, detached, charitable, humble or even recollected, obedient, chaste or poor in spirit. These virtues, if they are deeply rooted, certainly show whether he is open to grace. But what the priest has to verify in this instance is something more precise and delicate: whether there is an internal grace calling him to the life of a priest or religious and not simply to a fully Christian life in the world.

Such an examination, as has been shown at the beginning of this chapter, can only arrive at an affirmative conclusion after a considerable lapse of time: this is evident.

The life of a diocesan priest, just as much as that of a religious, only assumes its definitive aspect after ordination or final vows. While candidates are undergoing their period of formation, the environment in which they are developing and the work assigned to them have a very different character from what they will meet with in their ministries. They are followed closely, surrounded with care, lavishly supplied with counsels and advice and given only certain measures of responsibility. That is all quite normal. All the same they will one day find themselves left to their own resources and faced with their own responsibilities, particularly in the so-called active forms of life. They will have to put their maturity, initiative, zeal and discretion to the test without the rewards of encouragement or any call to order, and without being armed with a ready-made programme or a carefully worked out line of conduct.

For all this it is not impossible to verify the effects of grace after two or three years of formation. Before entry, however, the undertaking is more hazardous, unless the candidates are getting on for twenty-five. Indeed, adolescence is normally subject to so many upheavals that the facts it provides are expressions of the fluctuations inseparable from this age rather than personally assumed tendencies. In any case the priest responsible should not forget that his verification has to do with the real effects of grace and not with theoretical knowledge about it.

The life of prayer and the life of faith

All the elements of spiritual life, without exception, lend themselves to this kind of investigation, but there are some which reveal more, particularly the life of prayer and the practical understanding of the truths of faith.

These two aspects have been reflected on both spiritually and theologically by the Church for two thousand years. Any priest can compare his personal experience in these fields with writings of supreme value which will put him in direct contact with the substantial experience of the saints and the lucid thinking of the theologians. In these works he will find sure teaching on which to base his discernment, once he has become aware of its roots in his own personal life. In them he will find guides and landmarks, criteria and norms.

And then, these two aspects are of prime importance in the life of anyone who wants to devote himself entirely to God. They express in a very real way his aspirations and desires, and give proof of whether or not he is capable of fitting authentically (i.e. in accordance with the Church's teaching and experience) into the priestly or religious life.

The priest who undertakes to test these aspects in candidates who are relatively young or not far advanced in their formation may be helped by keeping the following points in mind.

As to prayer, which is the life of the soul, he can ask: Is it an exercise imposed from without; or does it proceed from an inward urge, so that he must adopt his own personal attitude towards it?—Is his prayer simply an asking for favours, or is it also, and primarily, a giving of self?—Is it a search for sensible consolations or emotionally felt desires, or does it try to find God, even in renunciation and aridity? Is it something static which fastens on to past experiences, or something alive and dynamic which goes forth into the future?—Does it follow the ups and downs of external circumstances or is it deeply rooted?

It is not uncommon to find cases where the motivation had remained doubtful and yet the answers to these questions all pointed in the same direction. Such a convergence is revealing and removes all doubts.

In the same way an attempt could be made to throw light on the candidate's attitude to the revelations of faith. Does he understand what he is saying when he talks about God, Christ, the Blessed Virgin and the saints, or does he allow his imagination to indulge in more or less pious flights of fancy?—Do spiritual truths, which he may well be fond of talking about, have any effective meaning for him and his behaviour, or are they merely abstract considerations and perhaps disordered ones?—Does he refer to some experience which has helped to form his judgment or does he confine everything to what he has been told and perhaps has heard repeatedly? Does he manage to form his own outlook from the whole corpus of revealed truths, or is he left cold by certain points and fascinated by others?

Once again, perfection should not be demanded at the very outset of the spiritual life. A thorough examination of conscience will reveal insufficiencies and gaps in all of us. But where a doubtful or insufficient motivation goes together with non-existent or purely formal prayer and a completely exterior or perhaps fanciful understanding of the truths of faith, there can be no further hesitation about passing a negative judgment. The priest consulted must in conscience let the candidate know.

An objection is sometimes raised to this procedure. It is true, it may be said, that a candidate does not give any definite signs of the presence of internal grace, but is it really certain that grace is not hidden deep down in his soul? To any suggestion of a lethargic grace there is only one retort: what right is there to speak of the presence of a grace which, by hypothesis, shows itself only in the absence of any effects? Make no mistake. In cases like this evasion is never justified; playing for time will only make the situation worse. It is vitally important to hasten on the awareness which the candidate has not so far been able to attain.

If, however, doubtful motivation is accompanied by a really discernible spiritual activity, the priest will have only one task: to help the candidate to go on with his spiritual experiment in order to make a more objective discernment possible. If this experiment takes place in the right setting, that of the discernment of spirits, there will be no need to fear that it will lead to any uneasiness or disorder. Objective information, reinforced by mutual confidence, will provide every opportunity of reaching a definite conclusion. If, though, the candidate is found to be incapable of assimilating the information and undergoing the trial and if, in spite of his good intentions and efforts, there are no signs of the life-giving action of God, it will be necessary to conclude that he has no vocation.

Before this section can be ended, a further danger must be pointed out. Spiritual directors and superiors sometimes allow themselves to be led into error by the tenacity with which certain candidates, whose unsuitability is obvious, defend their desire for the priesthood or religious life. Any desire, in fact, which does not take real difficulties into account, must be treated as suspect. This unreasoning desire is often quite senseless, since it is an obstinate rejection of reality and almost always springs from an immature attitude.

It is frequently met with among young people who have been taken up with it since their tenderest years. They have never had any doubt about it in spite of difficulty in studying or deviations of character, serious sexual failings or inveterate dishonesty. They give in at every setback, acquiesce in the habits they have formed, grieve about their lapses and do nothing about their dishonesty. All they have left is their desire, to which they hang on desperately because they have nothing else.

A negative judgment must be given, without any question at all; and it must be held to firmly in spite of lively protests or scarcely veiled threats. The only worthwhile help that can be offered is to suggest psychological treatment which may cure the pathological desire by helping towards greater maturity and a sense of personal responsibility.

The discernment of the internal grace of vocation demands insight, a knowledge of the objective criteria and a sure, delicate judgment on the part of the priest.

The obviously negative cases can be cleared up in a few conversations. For all the others it is necessary to have repeated contacts over a sufficiently long period of time, in order to be able to form an opinion about a candidate's dispositions and their development. A priest, even when he is a specialist, brought in for a passing consultation will only be able to form a valid judgment about the obviously negative cases.

The real evaluation and discernment of a positive internal vocation is above all a task for the spiritual director. Superiors cannot lose sight of this task of capital importance, although their hierarchical position hardly facilitates the complete frankness required for valid verification. This work can be done by the director under the seal of confession, while superiors can make only provisional assumptions.

This is why the director may not forget or make light of his responsibilities. It is for him to see that the candidate assimilates and puts into practice the principles taught him. If the candidate proves incapable of this, the director must enlighten him about his shortcomings and make him face up to the spiritual realities at stake. The director may even have to point out to him the insufficiency of his motives and the futility of his efforts, however well-intentioned. If the candidate refuses to draw the inevitable conclusions, the director will have to take a final step and oblige him to withdraw. Naturally the candidate has the right to submit all this to the superior as a check; he also has the right to go away for reasons given under the seal of confession without telling the superior of his motives. But in any case he cannot continue on the path he thinks right for himself against the formal notification from his director. And even if the director appears to him to be excessive, partial or not very competent,★ he is bound in conscience to communicate this notification either to the superior or to another spiritual director.

This touches on a very delicate and vital aspect of the problem: telling a candidate of the judgment formed about his vocation. The following chapter will be devoted to it.

★ His Holiness Pope Pius XI, in his encyclical *Ad Catholici Sacerdotii*, formally enjoins spiritual directors and confessors to see that unsuitable candidates do not go on towards the priesthood. Here are his own words: '... Confessors and spiritual directors could also be responsible for such a grave error; not indeed because they can take any outward action, since that is severely forbidden them by their most delicate office itself, and often also by the inviolable sacramental seal; but because they can have a great influence on the souls of the individual students ... Should the superiors, for whatever reason, take no action or show themselves weak, then especially should confessors and spiritual directors admonish the unsuited and unworthy, without any regard to human considerations, of their obligation to retire them while yet there is time. In this they should keep to the most secure opinion ... If sometimes they should not see so clearly that an obligation is to be imposed, let them at least use all the authority which springs from their office and the paternal affection they have for their spiritual sons, and so induce those who have not the necessary fitness to retire of their own free will.' And the instruction *Magna Equidem* emphasizes that in such a case it is sufficient for a candidate, even if a sub-deacon or deacon, to declare to his superior that in the opinion of his spiritual director or confessor he is unsuitable; and the superior will then have to take the necessary steps for laicizing him, without even making any further enquiries.

CHAPTER V

HOW DECISIONS ARE MADE KNOWN

THE normal development of a vocation does not, properly speaking, require any circumstantial communication of the decision, for the decision is made implicitly and results from the candidate's daily experience with the way of life.

1. THE IMPLICIT COMMUNICATION OF DECISIONS

If everything goes smoothly, superiors do not express any major objection concerning the candidate's aptitudes and spiritual directors do not indicate any serious short-coming as to internal vocation. Positively, they encourage the candidate to continue on the path he has chosen, and their remarks or recommendations are essentially about points which will ensure an ever more complete self-offering. At the major steps forward (admission to the noviciate or seminary, going on to philosophy or theology, renovation of vows, minor and major orders), notifying the candidate of his admission to the next grade is equivalent to imparting a positive judgment on his vocation.

Thus in the majority of cases this intimation is made without any systematic examination or setting out of reasons. The candidate, happy in his new life, is entitled to consider the approbation of his superiors and directors as a confirmation of the authenticity of his desire and will to commit himself. There is no problem here.

The situation changes completely once hesitation makes itself felt. Any hesitation at all poses a question and demands its answer. Once that has happened it is not permissible to avoid a systematic examination or to refuse to make known the resulting judgment. Breaking the news can be a very delicate business in many cases.

It may be the candidate who feels hesitant, without there being any doubt on the part of the responsible authorities—this happens particularly when the aptitudes seem satisfactory all round. Or it may lie with the authorities, without any worry on the part of the candidate. And finally and most dramatically, it can happen when the superior or director are convinced of the lack of vocation, without the candidate falling in with their views. We will look into each of these three eventualities in order to show how they should be dealt with.

2. AN EXPLICIT DECISION ON THE INITIATIVE OF THE CANDIDATE

The uncertainty may lie with the candidate: perhaps he has met some difficulty, is ill at ease over something, and feels anxious, unsettled or completely confused. Quite rightly he wonders whether everything is going as it should or whether he has made a mistake. We must take care not to misinterpret this hesitancy. It could easily be the beginning of a deeper awareness: the value, purpose and responsibilities of a call from God are more clearly seen; in consequence the inevitable shortcomings are more sharply felt. It may also be the first sign that he has no vocation: between the ideal he has set before himself and the life he is actually leading, he notes a discrepancy which has hitherto escaped him.

Whatever the origin of his irresolution, his superior and directors would be well advised to accept it as a fact to be reckoned with. To reject it out of hand as a temptation, to tell the candidate to take no notice, without examining its significance, would be harmful whatever the case. If this is the beginning of a deeper awareness, then they are shutting the door on the spiritual enrichment which might have come from it; if, on the other hand, it is a negative sign, there is danger of letting a candidate keep going on the wrong path. As soon as any irresolution which is at all persistent shows itself, they must act decisively and face up to the difficulty without fear or perturbation. Its spontaneous appearance indicates that the candidate is sufficiently mature to embark on a methodical examination. If the various stages of the examination are explained to him and have a close bearing on his personal experience, he will find it easier to look for and discover the revealing signs of God's action in his spiritual behaviour. It is on such occasions that the findings of an examination really can be taken to heart, just because of the trial the candidate is enduring.

The superior or director who are called to the rescue have no right to refuse to accept the call, under the pretext of setting the candidate's mind at rest. Even supposing that they succeed in doing so, it would be an uneasy calm, with only two possible meanings: either the subject has given up the struggle or he is deluding himself. In both cases the opportunity to make any profitable and remedial contribution through a personal solution of the candidate's problem is irretrievably lost. A deceptive attitude has been created and sooner or later the day of reckoning will come. As always in the spiritual life, it is essential to have the courage to make a person face up to the inevitable crises of growth, and by quiet encouragement to bring him to see things prudently but fearlessly.

Superiors and directors should not think that they are thereby surrendering their initiative. On such occasions, they must be able to answer conscientiously for a candidate's aptitudes, but they should word their answer in such a way that the candidate does not see it as a formal injunction or command. Otherwise they run the risk of intimidating nervous or scrupulous candidates, who are already tempted to put themselves entirely into the hands of others. A vocation can never be imposed from outside, even if it is really present; the assent given to it sets a man free only if it stems from a personal commitment, freely consented to.

The candidate's uncertainty must be respected; it should be taken seriously and seen for what it really is, in the growth to spiritual maturity. Whatever conclusion is arrived at, it can be turned to the advantage of a more mature and personal commitment. Those in authority who have experience and clear-sightedness will not be surprised by such a crisis, even if it is a violent one, since it is a sign of life and growth.

3. AN EXPLICIT DECISION ON THE INITIATIVE OF THE AUTHORITIES

Some candidates never cast any doubts on their vocation, yet those responsible are very worried at their doings. Their lack of discipline, their irregularity and instability hold no promise for the future, and are often betrayed by troublesome excesses or singular behaviour. Here again there should be no yielding to the temptation to sugar the pill. If doubts are objectively justified they must be made known to the candidate clearly and without evasion. But any observations made should be put in the right setting—that of the spiritual discernment of vocation.

Superiors—and even directors—may be inclined to take the easy way out. Rather than saddle themselves with a careful examination which takes time and patience, they are sometimes content to demand an outward falling into line: the gossip, who is trying to compensate for his own inner emptiness, is told not to talk so much; the idler, who only knows by hearsay the meaning of serving God, is told to work harder; the grumbler is told to be more pleasant; the moody man is told to go steady and the rebel to be content with things as he finds them.

Where it is a question of minor faults in a candidate whose authentic vocation gives no cause for doubt, such demands are not unreasonable. But when it is a matter of inveterate behaviour, these otherwise quite legitimate demands are unlikely to effect any solution. There is, indeed, the danger of adding to the evils to be eradicated the much worse ones of dissimulation and hypocrisy. The dissimulation is not necessarily conscious, but the candidate feels driven to it, without really knowing why. He may feel that he is picked on, and think or see himself under close surveillance. Convinced that he is in the right place, he simply does his best to give no further cause for comment. He has been asked to attend to his external attitude, this is all he feels he has to conform to, and he has not the slightest sense of personal involvement. Indeed, he may come to think of the things that have been said and the measures taken as vexatious, as well as excessive and unfair. The authorities will congratulate themselves, perhaps, on having nothing more to complain about from the candidate who was causing them such worry. But can it be said that any positive result or any real improvement has been achieved?

Sometimes, too, the demands made of the candidate are out of all proportion. His whole spiritual effort is concentrated entirely on this outward behaviour, which is in no way connected with the fullness of the spiritual life. In order to avoid the disaster of a dismissal which he thinks is hanging over him, he sometimes brings off a considerable feat, and succeeds by superhuman efforts to conform outwardly to the injunctions received. It need not be said that there is no really lasting effect, and this will be proved by the reappearance of the difficulties, which one had hoped to eliminate, after his admission to vows or the reception of orders.

Where it is felt to be necessary, those responsible have to make clear demands, but these are better expressed in general terms so that candidates can prove, by finding out for themselves how to put them into practice, that they are capable of personal initiative.

It should be noted once more that the considerations set down here are not concerned with everyday disciplinary demands which are inherent in any community life. Anyone who has lived in a community knows that the observation of silence, the order of the day, and exercises in common must regularly be brought to mind and commended during retreats or days of recollection. The spiritual world is not immune from human weakness. But when the behaviour of a candidate is giving worry, any results obtained by repeated insistence, which the candidate has accepted with a bad grace or considered unwarranted, must be regarded with suspicion.

Any reservation on the part of the candidate or of those responsible calls for a methodical examination, carried out with mutual agreement. Those responsible must work out the processes to be followed, the elements to be examined and the values to be recognized. The candidate must take the principles to heart with a view to applying them intelligently to his own personal experience.

When the issue is approached in this straightforward way, it can usually be resolved by a clear-cut decision confirmed by both parties. Whatever the decision may be—to go on or to leave—it has always a positive value. It results, in fact, from the conscious, deliberate acceptance of the will of God. The discernment, accepted and carried out with full understanding, always brings very real advantages: a genuine personal attitude, renunciation of selfish, self-centred desires and conformity to the Lord's call.

4. INFORMING A CANDIDATE WHO IS UNDER AN ILLUSION

All is well so long as the candidate shows himself capable of a genuine and disinterested commitment to the objective demands of the life he is leading. Unfortunately the necessary maturity and detachment are not always present. What is to be done when a candidate who is manifestly unsuitable or simply has no vocation cannot bring himself to face up to the facts?

This is a painful situation and forces those responsible to accept their duty. Conscious of the mandate received from the Church and therefore from God, they have to make their decision known to the candidate; and no consideration can let them off this duty.★ But it is advisable for them to bear in mind certain factors which are often at work in the stubborn candidate, so that they do not make his condition any worse. His reticence generally springs from a lack of perspective about vocation itself or about the decision which bears upon it.

In the first place it is important to explain to him patiently and

---

★ All the official documents are quite explicit about the exclusion of doubtful cases. Superiors, spiritual directors and confessors are not entitled to turn a blind eye to an objectively founded doubt either by the possible shortage of vocations (*Ad Catholici Sacerdotii*), or sympathy for unfortunate candidates (the same encyclical describes such sympathy as *impia pietas*), or outstanding qualities in all other respects but the one which is lacking (*Magna Equidem*). As long as there is an unresolved doubt they must decide against: '. . . They should keep to the most secure opinion, which in this case is the one most in favour of the penitent, for it saves him from a step which could be for him eternally fatal' (*Ad Catholici Sacerdotii*). Article 34, ¶2, of the *Statuta Generalia* states just as clearly the same requirement, to which there can be no exceptions. The letter of the S. Congregation of Seminaries (27th September, 1960) to the hierarchy justifies this 'tutiorism' at great length (Cf. note, p. 133).

clearly the specific character of vocation, which is a free and gratuitous call from God, not the fulfilment of a more or less self-interested desire. To this should be added the providential character of inaptitudes and insufficient motivations. It should be urged that such indications are negative in relation to vocations in the strict sense, but positive as to commitment to Christian life in the world. Above all an attempt must be made to make him aware of this positive value. An examination which concludes with the absence of vocation does not mean either disgrace or expulsion.

But an immature candidate often gets the impression that all religious values are crumbling away under him when he discards his religious habit. He feels he has been led to his mistaken decision through faulty convictions. The life of a religious or priest had seemed the only valid and worthwhile state, and ordinary Christian life had lost all its value for him. In order to help him to a genuine acceptance of the step he has to take, he must be enabled to see the values of his new life. Indeed, generosity, self-forgetfulness, helping one's neighbour, love of God and sanctity are not the exclusive preserve of religious and priests. It is advisable to tell him this. Even better help him to appreciate it fully by referring to examples he cannot look down upon: those of his parents, his married brothers and sisters, unselfish friends and practising Christians.

Where his motivation has been self-centred, the step the candidate must take is complicated by his having to confront the risks and perils he had tried to avoid. This suggests immediately that he has a weak character or a timid nature. He must be given support, but this must be done by encouraging, enlightening and sustaining him in his personal efforts rather by trying to do it all for him.

Material help can be given him, and superiors usually give it unhesitatingly; he can also be helped to find a job. But if he is willing and able to find his own way, no watchful eye should be kept over him, as he may feel that this is irksome and interfering. But if he is helpless and perplexed, he should be assisted to find his feet without any more intervention than is strictly necessary. This does not mean losing interest in him, or failing in any duty, but rather that he is being offered every opportunity of personal achievement. In fact, if he is to readjust himself fully, he will as soon as possible have to break off all links with the superiors on whom he was depending and the members of the community to which he belonged. The longer he has been in religious life or the seminary, the more important it is to see that a clean break is made.

While we are still on this point, let us suggest that he should have no further contacts with his former companions and that he should change his spiritual director and immediately adopt a lay spirituality.

The break with his old companions is most important. Anyone who leaves must be freed from all hindrances so that he can look into the future without being weighed down by the past. A ship which leaves port must cut all its cables.

The change of spiritual director is necessary for the same reason. To change, but not to do without a director. He must find out not only how to lead a full life in the world and find a regular job; it is also important for him to lead an intense spiritual life there: but it must be adapted to his changed circumstances.

Now it is obvious that what he has learnt and even put into practice in his spirituality was designed as part of his life as a religious or seminarist. If he is given no help or enlightenment he is liable, after discarding his habit, to throw overboard all spiritual exercise and rest content with being present at Sunday mass and going less and less frequently to confession.

Others react in the opposite direction. Wanting to remain fundamentally directed towards God, they lay down an order of the day based entirely on the one they have been used to. The time given to the exercises is necessarily reduced, but they scrupulously maintain periods of meditation, examination of conscience, recitation of the office, and so on. With some difficulty they remain faithful to practices which prove to be purely external. The time given over to the various exercises is shortened again, but they dare not leave any of them out. Anxiety grips them and they feel they are sliding into indifference. They work against the clock to fit everything in; inspiration gets lost and all relish with it.

If their spiritual director or the priest they talk to accepts them without brutally rejecting their ill-advised resolutions, he will gradually bring them to understand that they must find a spiritual life which, while still fed on their aspirations, seeks an adapted form of expression.

If such a solution is presented to them, they will generally accept it with relief. They will be glad to replace the truncated meditation, examination and office with exercises which mean something to them. They should be induced to turn their attention to morning prayers, an offering of the coming day, prayers in the evening, a recapitulation and thanksgiving. It might be suggested that they should recollect themselves during the prayers they make normally, e.g. before and after meals. They should make Sunday mass a prayer in which they unite themselves with all Christian people. They should use their zeal for serving the Lord through giving themselves to their new occupations and trying in them to conform themselves to the will of God. Without any difficulty they will find many occasions for practising patience, humility and charity.

By directing his charge in this way the director will ward off many disappointments and disillusionments. With even greater reason must he formally advise a person coming back into the world against binding himself by a private vow either of obedience to his director or of chastity. In the unanimous opinion of theologians such practices are only to be allowed with the greatest caution. Those who have left a religious house or seminary are often tempted to turn to such a vow as a substitute.

It is the young women rather than the men who are inclined to seek refuge or compensation in this. It may even happen at first that everything seems to be going well. They remain in their family surroundings and go back to their old friends. Occasionally they perform some good work or other. But later, when their friends have married and their parents have died, they find themselves alone at the age of thirty-five or forty. Only then do they feel that their lives are without purpose and their hearts have dried up because their decision sprang from a human desire rather than from God's grace. They hesitate to set themselves free of their obligations for fear of losing esteem in their own eyes and in those of their director. And it is too late to start life all over again.

Both authorities and candidates gain by facing serenely and objectively whatever reservations come to light. An unacknowledged fear which pretends it knows no uncertainty engenders indefinable uneasiness and vague anxieties.

Courage and insight are needed. All the anxieties which make themselves felt must be seen in the spiritual and supernatural light of what vocation is. Truth alone brings freedom: truth unreserved and accepted by all. Neither the hesitant candidate nor the person who has been 'turned out' is really helped unless all the authorities and advisers let themselves be guided by this same spirit of God. His life-giving inspiration rekindles their generosity, which any abrupt check might well have stifled.

It is not without reason that we have laid so much insistence on the fearless adoption of a personal attitude. So often complaints are raised about the immaturity of seminarists and young religious even at the end of their years of formation.

Superiors, concerned about their task as educators and forma-tive influences, strive to find opportunities to give their subjects a sense of their responsibilities. To this end they multiply social studies, catechetical instruction, excursions into apostolic work, mission-camps, etc.

This is all very praiseworthy and deserving. But it is obvious that none of these initiatives come anywhere near the responsibil-ities taken on by a young man and woman working together to set up a home, and leaving their family surroundings to create an independent life. They are not asked to reject the past or to forget the examples and lessons they have received, but to fit all they have acquired into a personal confrontation with the realities of life.

It is surely desirable for seminarists and young religious to be urged to come to terms with reality in the same way, but on the spiritual level. They should be asked—and therefore allowed—to fit the instruction they have received and the formation im-parted to them into a personal confrontation with the spiritual realities of their interior life.

Heavy burdens will soon be laid on them. The responsibilities of the priestly ministry, the formation of youth, and preaching the Gospel are serious in a different way from those of setting up a home. How may they best be prepared to direct others? Surely by teaching them to direct themselves, by allowing them the op-portunity of facing on their own the inevitable upheavals of spirit-ual growth and appealing to their judgment in matters of con-science. There must be supervision, obviously. But it must further their sense of personal involvement and not act as a substitute for them through excessive caution or concern.

CHAPTER VI

DISCERNING VOCATIONS IN PRACTICE

WE have now studied the constituent elements of vocations and discernment. But the subject is not yet exhausted. Every vocation, in fact, must be sought in its framework of an individual life, for it is subject to the laws of growth contained in each person. It is worth examining more closely the normal stages of this development.

1. THE ACTUAL STAGES IN A VOCATION

The influences, first of the earliest years of family upbringing and subsequently of school life and social environment, shape the character by action and reaction. The ground is thus prepared for the nurture of a vocation. The child starts to realize himself as an individual, a person, living in close contact with others; he becomes increasingly aware of his personal relations with other people and with God.

One actual circumstance or another in the exterior or interior life (the force of another's example, becoming aware of a religious need or some spiritual impetus, a difficulty which forces him to adopt a personal attitude) will first prompt the idea of a vocation. This idea may undergo eclipses, especially if it is formed before the upheavals of puberty. Normally it remains for some time in the realm of vague possibilities unless particular circumstances, such as admission to a minor seminary, crystallize it provisionally. The principal element in these years of emergent vocation is the slow progression by which the vague idea takes the form of a personal call.

It is then that the adolescent seeks means of fulfilment, without usually having any very clear idea of where or how he will finish up. Gradually he comes to see the outlines of the sort of life he wants to embrace. Sometimes this search proceeds smoothly, because from the outset he has chanced across the form of life which seems to correspond to his expectations and aspirations; sometimes he encounters many setbacks because fulfilment seems to slip out of his grasp.

But whatever avenues of approach he treads, the decision to follow one definite path must be qualified: 'I have made up my mind, provided that this path corresponds to my true calling.' This qualification is almost always only inferred, but is nonetheless real. On the part of superiors also, admission to the years of formation must be similarly qualified, but usually the condition is equally rarely made explicit: 'We admit him provided he proves satisfactory.'

From then on it is a matter of dealing with a vocation in full growth. The candidate can judge for himself what the life proposed to him is about, by living it from within. By daily experience he becomes aware of its meaning, its value and its demands. The superiors also can take their time in seeing how the candidate develops and whether his exterior attitude and spiritual growth are leading him to an even more complete identification with the type of life he has embraced.

Finally, the intention of the candidate who commits himself with his eyes open, and the call of the superiors who with full knowledge of the case invite him in the name of God, come together and definitively consecrate the vocation at the time of ordination or final vows. Now it is a fully evolved vocation.

In the actual course of such an individual spiritual progress several decisive stages stand out: possibly entry to the 'école apostolique' or junior seminary (the humanities), entry to the noviciate or seminary (philosophy), and admission to final commitment. And it may happen that after this final commitment doubts about vocation may arise, either as an interior crisis or from exterior influences.

It is during these four periods that appeal is most likely to be made to superiors, directors or advisers for a decision. The general principles and practical directives we have already discussed indicate the line to be followed and the help to be given, and we will not go over this ground again. But it does not seem out of place to show their scope in greater detail and examine their practical application for each of these stages, since the age of the candidates, their individual situation, their experience of life, their religious knowledge and their first-hand awareness of spiritual things vary considerably at each stage. All these factors must be weighed and seen in their relative importance.

2. ADMISSION TO THE JUNIOR OR MINOR SEMINARY

Junior seminaries admit boys from twelve to fourteen years of age, minor seminaries provide a two year preparatory course for the senior, or major seminary, for boys who may not have been to the junior seminary. Living as boarders and forming a more or less homogeneous group, they have the opportunity of pursuing their studies in humanities as a step towards possible entry to the seminary or noviciate. The youth of these boarders sets the problem of how to discern their vocation.

What is about to be said on this subject applies also to the junior-ates for brothers or the training colleges for 'lay' sisters, which receive boys or girls, generally from fourteen to sixteen, who have a desire to enter religion. Although the studies are different, the purpose is the same and they should be looked at in the same way.

Houses for late vocations are rather different. They undertake to teach Latin, often in record time, to older people, usually from seventeen to twenty-five. For admission to these houses, reference should be made to the details given subsequently in this chapter when admission to the seminary or noviciate are dealt with.

Before or during the age of puberty there is very little scope for decision about the vocations of children admitted to the junior or minor seminary. Certainly the aptitudes are fundamentally present, but sudden changes are always possible. Some of them seem very difficult or not very gifted, but get over this admirably, to everyone's surprise; others seem very promising but cause cruel disillusion several years later. Interior vocation also eludes all investigation. Grace does, indeed, start working from the earliest years, and sure signs of it can often be observed, but it is difficult, if not impossible, to make out its long-term significance. No one will venture to predict what the attitude of any particular boy or girl may be when the time comes for them to decide about a definite personal commitment.★

★ This is not to exclude the possibility of a systematic examination of candidates even before entry to the minor seminary or junior seminary. Th. del Arroyo describes the minor seminary which has been instituted in the diocese of Saragossa (Spain). In this case it will be noted that it involves a term of probation, which permits an observation of the general behaviour of the boys concerned and the elimination of those who, because of health, character, or previous education, do not appear suitable for the studies or the formation in the minor seminary. It is more a question of a judicious preselection than of a real discernment of vocations. This does not detract from the worthwhileness of the experiment and the results obtained seem to be good. Cf. Th. DEL ARROYO, *Une expérience de discernement,* supplement of *Vie Spirituelle,* no. 49, 1959, pp. 183-202.

Should we then admit, or even invite, every candidate who presents himself, without making any effort to distinguish between them? This would be going too far. All things considered, it would appear both sufficient and necessary for two conditions to be fulfilled: does the child really want to enter the school with the distant but serious prospect of becoming a priest or religious? and has he the aptitudes on which to base some hope of satisfactory development? Let us now consider more closely this desire and these aptitudes.

Freedom to be safeguarded

The desire of the boy or girl must be sincere. We can hardly expect more than this. The rightness of the child's intention can not validly be put to the test, for this would presuppose an explicit knowledge of religious things and a first-hand experience of spiritual ones as well as a growing personal maturity, which are not usual at the age of twelve or fourteen.

Likewise it is vitally important that the child should not feel his admission as a duty forced on him or a path to be followed unwillingly. Outward acquiescence does not always express what is in the depths of a child's soul. More frequently than might be thought, children feel themselves trapped. Those who invite or urge them to enter a junior seminary or 'école apostolique' do not always make sufficient allowance for their mentality.

The invitation or encouragement of the parish priest, anxious to foster vocations, and the consent of parents, happy to give a son or daughter to the Lord, assumes for children the appearance of a wish they cannot get away from, a command they must obey. Has it not been drilled into them that the priest speaks in God's name and that one must never disobey one's parents? The priest in charge of vocations, to whom a good boy or an exemplary mass-server has been pointed out, is apt to appeal to his generosity, his good character and his good nature: 'Surely he wants to give himself entirely to God?' The boy gets a distinct impression that if he puts up any excuse for refusing the idea which is described in such glistening terms, he will be letting the side down. If his apparent goodness springs from a timid nature, he will think himself in the wrong to offer a refusal whose unfortunate consequences he dreads.

When adults are not sufficiently attentive to what they say and how they say it, the children, for all these reasons and many others besides, will say 'yes' with apparent joy or even with genuine good grace. In fact, they are bitterly regretting what is being left behind or suffer very greatly at being unable to fulfil a dream for the future which they are secretly cherishing, because it is too beautiful or private for them to breathe a word about it.

After that their lives are liable to be marked by an indefinable nostalgia, whose origins are swallowed up in the past, but whose effects are blatantly obvious. All sorts of compensations are looked for: refuge in day-dreaming, the need for kindness and affection, an irresistible seeking after external successes, and a tendency to avail themselves of the good things of life (good food, good living, good comfort . . .) We sometimes wonder where such desires come from, but often it is only nature taking its revenge for an unwilling sacrifice.

Aptitudes to be verified

The aptitudes of the children in question, as has already been said, cannot be assessed with certainty. Their character, talents, and capacities of every kind will show only with time.

Attention, however, must always be paid to negative indications or serious drawbacks, whether they are mainly personal or derive mainly from the family background. Alcoholism, dissoluteness, quarrelling and serious character failings on the part of the parents have a marked effect on the psychological development during the first years of life. Education and training given in adolescence are not enough to neutralize or cancel previous development. It is not possible to build on sand, even if the materials used are of excellent quality.

It will often not be possible at the beginning to appraise the damage done to the child in question by the family background. If it seems likely that there are grounds for solid hopes in such a case, the candidate may be admitted, but an attempt must be made from the time he arrives to check what havoc the influences he has undergone have caused.

It can be seen that even confining ourselves to these two points it is scarcely an easy matter to discern a vocation. This should not be too great a cause for alarm. If a careful watch is kept on these two points there is no objection to admitting any genuine candidate, without going into too detailed an examination, which could never be conclusive. We must always, of course, make the provision that he should find the atmosphere in the junior or minor seminary favourable to a normal development to maturity. These institutions are only justified if they gradually make possible a decision which it was not possible to reach before entry.

Conditions to be fulfilled

To this end the responsible authorities must create a 'normal' environment, permit natural psychological development and ensure the possibility of reinforcing the initial decision, reconsidering it and even freely revoking it.★

★ In *Menti Nostrae*, Pope Pius XII speaks at some length about the formation of young people who are being prepared for the priesthood from the age of twelve to fourteen. He emphasizes several points which have guided the statements made in this book: 'their life should correspond, as far as possible, with the normal life of boys'; the superiors will 'gradually ... relax the strictness of the surveillance and the various

The environment can be called normal if it does not cut the youngsters off from their families, which are and always will be the natural surroundings for adolescents, and if it offers them, with an eye to their future, studies equivalent to those carried out by other boys and girls of their own age. In short, there must be no question of turning them into children 'apart' or 'not like others'. No spiritual regime, either monastic or clerical, should be imposed on them, for it would not be in the least suited to their mentality; there should be no soutane or religious habit which might single them out in the eyes of others.

Sending them back regularly to their families can sometimes be difficult because of distance, but it is indispensable for this to be done three times a year (a fortnight at Christmas and Easter and at least six weeks in the summer).

Equivalent studies suppose also equivalent qualifications obtained at the end of them. If the studies organized at the school do not lead to an officially recognized certificate which allows the pupils to go on to higher studies or a career, even a manual one, there is a danger of forcing them to continue towards the priesthood or in religious life for worldly motives. If these studies are lessened or cut down so as not to put off certain candidates, a real danger is incurred of forming priests who are not up to the standard required for their apostolic work, particularly in intellectual matters.

A normal environment creates favourable conditions for the psychological development of the pupils. Attention must also be paid to the attitude taken by directors and superiors, for it is their

---

controls. By this means they will induce self-discipline and a sense of personal responsibility'; 'when young men have been educated—especially from their tender years—in places somewhat too secluded from normal social intercourse, they will find some difficulty afterwards in adjusting themselves to the ways not only of the educated but also of the ordinary people'; 'in literary and scientific studies our future priests should at least not yield place to lay boys who are taking the same course'.

job to respect the normal maturing of character as well as to further it.

It should never be forgotten that maturity is not so much the result of outward constraint as the outcome of personal commitments. A difficulty overcome is a guarantee for the future, while any shrinking from it carries great risks. If aspirants have desires for independence or feelings of rebellion, sexual curiosities or affection for one of the other sex, criticisms of the regime or boredom with their exercises of piety, these should be understood, accepted and explained to them in a positive way which will help them to form their own opinions. Otherwise the only outcome is to subdue insubordinate and rebellious characters or bring the undisciplined and idle into some sort of line. This is no preparation for the personal responsibilities of apostolic work and the freedom which will be plentifully theirs after their training.

If a boy of fifteen is sent away because he realizes with embarrassment that he has several times chatted with the girl at the shoe-shop when collecting repaired shoes and admits he is in love with her, and is then cited as an example of infidelity to his 'vocation', it is probable that the minds and hearts of the others will be distorted, making them perhaps turn their affections upon their companions or think of tendencies, in themselves healthy and normal, as sinful.

The possibility of reinforcing, reconsidering and revoking their decision must be fully safeguarded for the young. It is not sufficient for superiors to proclaim that they are not holding anyone back and that those who want to leave may do so (at their own risk, it is implied). The attitude of the authorities can be very questionable. It is often clearly hinted that to leave is infidelity, cowardice, betrayal, and contemptible. This attitude may hold the timid and pusillanimous, but it exasperates those who are generous and decisive.

Children who have doubts or reservations should be treated

patiently and impartially, and helped to see in these a providential opportunity to reach a better understanding of the life best suited to them. If superiors and directors leave the door open for a negative decision, they are at the same time creating a favourable atmosphere for a free and positive decision. For the younger ones it may be best to forewarn them about onslaughts of moodiness and hasty decisions. When they are a little older the best results are obtained by stressing the underlying reasons for their reservations and objections. In doing so, they should be urged to form an objective judgment and decide for themselves. If, in such a case, an aspirant decides not to come back again, the authorities must not lose interest in him, under the pretext that enough time and money have already been wasted to no avail: the very fact that they admitted him means that they have contracted a duty in conscience. They must make smooth his return to his family and see that he settles down, especially if the family fails to give sufficient help. On occasion, admirable help is given by associations of the old pupils of such schools.

When all these conditions are fulfilled, the very atmosphere in the schools will override most of the objections sometimes raised against them, and with good reason. These institutions will then contribute to the end which justifies them: to provide the Church with recruits from among young people whose material circumstances are less favourable than others, but who are gifted and evidently called by the Lord.

3. ENTRY TO THE SEMINARY OR NOVICIATE

Candidates to the seminary or noviciate are at least seventeen years old, and their maturity may already be considerable; their characters are more stable, their gifts and talents more apparent and their religious attitude is deepening.

So it is now possible to make a thorough examination, particularly of their aptitudes; their motivation can also be checked. But the result will still be conclusive only in obviously negative cases: i.e. with candidates whose motivation is patently insufficient. For all the others it is necessary to wait and see. It is very often essential to pass through the first years of formation before confirming or dispelling any doubts and bringing clear indications to light.

What has been said in previous chapters about discerning vocations applies here; all that remains now is to focus attention on a few subtle points. How important they are, and what repercussions they may have, sometimes escapes the perspicacity of those responsible for enlightening candidates about their intentions.

Right intention on the part of the candidate

Any priest asked to handle a question of vocation must be convinced that the most important factor in the work of discernment is that of right intention. He is in an especially good position to form a judgment. But how often, unfortunately, does one hear the judgment: 'This young man would make a good priest, that girl would make an excellent nun', referring only to aptitudes. This is to be guilty of a grave error of judgment.

When carrying out this examination of motivation the priest will nearly always find human motives intervening. There is no reason for concern so long as these reasons, insufficient in themselves or unsuited to the ends in view, do not override all others. Certainly they should not be exaggerated in such a way as to alarm the candidate. They must simply be put in their right place, so that the candidate, by living his vocation, can purify his intentions on these points.

But if the motivation remains purely human (desire for security, personal fulfilment, refuge from the responsibilities of life, and the like), the candidate must be brought gradually to a personal awareness of this. To present him with a verdict usually only leads him to stiffen in his attitude and hang on all the more obstinately to his idea. Indeed, it is to take the ground very suddenly from under his feet. This is the time when the adviser must unflinchingly have recourse to a judicious technique in his interviews with him, with the aim of rebuilding his personality little by little by dismantling the false superstructures he has erected. If he goes about it correctly, the adviser will rarely have to take the extreme measure of telling the candidate that he must in conscience reveal his motivations to the appropriate authority.

Subjective reactions on the part of the consultant priest

But the adviser must do more than just help the candidate to be more objective. He is himself exposed to the danger of letting subjective factors influence his judgment and unduly influence the candidate's future. He must be on the watch for these personal reactions, especially as they are so often unconscious or very nearly so.

He should not let himself be carried away by the understandable but all too human desire of seeing a pleasant or gifted candidate join a community of which he himself is a member. It is not rare to see young people without a vocation join because they are urged to do so by an 'admirer'. It is even quite frequent to come across young people whose vocation is quite genuine but who are put off by the importunate, over-human insistence of a priest who is zealous but has little idea of his own motives. In the first case, the young man is deflected from what he should really be doing. He will (it is to be hoped) return to this, but there is a danger that he will become embittered. In the second case, the insistence may make him react by refusing his vocation, either for the time being or for good. Sometimes the effect is not so disastrous and is confined to a persistent doubt and a vague uneasiness, which are all the more difficult to cure in candidates whose aptitudes and internal vocation are beyond all doubt, if its causes are not recognized. In these cases a very long and patient reviewing of motivation will have to be undertaken.

Just as dangerous is the negative attitude of a priest towards a candidate he finds rather uninteresting, either for objective reasons, such as mediocre gifts and talents, or through incompatibility of temperament. The young man has a distinct, if subconscious, feeling that his rejection is motivated by inadequate or secondary reasons. For this reason the priest consulted should beware of putting his advice in a negative way, such as: 'You're none too brilliant at study, so don't take up anything that needs a long and difficult training!' Then there is a danger of establishing the candidate in a false conviction: that of a vocation on the cheap. The adviser's task is essentially positive, and he should help the candidate discover the way in which his talents, even if mediocre, may be best employed in the Lord's service. The candidate will then be able to give of his best, without straining himself by quite disproportionate efforts which will sooner or later lead him to overwork or collapse.

Hesitant candidates

Sometimes hesitant, timid or scrupulous candidates more or less explicitly ask the priest to decide whether they have a vocation. As long as this means determining the positive factors and confirming the absence of indications to the contrary, the adviser cannot shirk the job, but the candidate's commitment must remain purely personal and the priest should abstain from substituting his own decision for that of the candidate.

If the candidate's state of mind is relatively healthy, a few conversations will be enough to give a satisfactory idea of the meaning, significance and necessity of a personal decision. He will then be in a position to act on his own initiative. If these conversations go on without any result, then there is a more or less serious psychological deficiency and it will be necessary to turn to a specialist, to establish the exact nature of the disturbance and give an opinion about the helpfulness of an appropriate course of treatment.

For a priest to act in the place of the candidate and vouch for him will only give rise to worse evils. The candidate will be committed to a life which is vitiated at the roots by a fatal aversion and handicapped for the rest of his life—and the trouble will usually get worse.

Even after a thorough examination many cases remain in doubt. The retarded psychological development of some candidates and the vacillations of a still unformed personality in others do not allow an absolutely certain diagnosis.

To obviate the drawbacks of an examination from which little or no conclusion can be reached, certain orders set a definite age limit for admission. Candidates may not offer themselves until they are twenty-one or have completed their military service.

In many countries the definite choice of a career is made, in practice, at the end of secondary education. This custom leads to the difficulty of one or two years' gap. It is even more awkward to have a break between the last year at the 'école apostolique' and entry to the noviciate.

When there is uncertainty or doubt it is better, ideally speaking, for the candidate to delay his entry. His decision will be better able to mature if he takes a job, follows some profession or goes on with higher studies. The practical advantages of a delay should not be forgotten. And when a persistent doubt is evident, it is only right and wise to suggest, and even to insist on, a delay.

Does this run the risk of seeing vocations become lost? The danger is minimal if the interruption is presented, not as a rejection or a vexatious measure, but as a time of maturing. If it is explained frankly to the candidate that he is being offered an opportunity of getting to know himself better and developing further, he will readily assent to the test and profit from it. His very acceptance of the proposal and the way he carries it out can give much useful information about his real dispositions. His progress should be followed, not in order to press him or supervise him, but to learn whether he is managing to develop by his own efforts and make up his own mind. A similar attitude is necessary when a superior or spiritual director discovers a lack of decisiveness in a candidate who has already been admitted to the seminary or noviciate.

4. THE YEARS OF FORMATION

A vocation, being a personal commitment to a particular form of life, must grow in depth and intensity. But such a growth does not proceed without jolts and collisions, and in this it follows the laws of all life. Sudden advances are followed by periods of lull, and apparent aridity precedes flowering. There is no need to worry about these vital rhythms in which untroubled joy alternates with distressing trials.

It is normal for problems to be raised by the need to face up to new situations or unexpected responsibilities during the years of formation. The move from philosophy to theology, military service, going from the noviciate to studies, the teaching experiment and the period of university studies are all new situations. The candidate is liable to lose his self-assurance. A new approach to the observance of regulations, a complete change of background, instruction in unfamiliar subjects, all demand from him an effort at self-adaptation. He must disengage the essential values of his spiritual life and religious aspirations if he is to maintain them without wavering. If he is capable of this, the adaptation will do no harm. The inevitable hesitations and uncertainties at the beginning will resolve themselves and give way to an untroubled assurance based on personal experience. Occasional failings should not cause surprise, for insofar as they make a deeper and more explicit understanding possible, they are beneficial.

Superiors, directors and consultant priests must disengage this positive aspect from the difficulties which arise.★ Sometimes there

---

★ The first part of the letter addressed to the hierarchy by the S. Congregation of Seminaries, dated 27th September 1960, deals exclusively with the selection of candidates during the years of formation. It is stated very insistently that this selection is one of the essential tasks before seminaries 'in which superiors receive a mandate from the authority of the Church to recognize those who are truly called by God ... Ecclesiastical authority has, therefore, the strict obligation of checking the authenticity of the divine call in all the students.... This verification begins at the first entry to the seminary and ends with admission to Orders in the positive cases; in the negative cases it ends in immediate dismissal once a practical judgment about the candidate's unsuitability has been formed' (first paragraph).

It is then stressed that a clear mind must be kept when considering qualities or capacities in isolation: 'The candidate's suitability must be judged as a whole, in all its aspects.' 'Certain brilliant people, for example, may immediately make the best impression; but since they often lack all reliability ... they will later be found unable to overcome the great difficulties of life ... On other occasions a careful examination may show how little justified is the esteem given to young people who appear very pious ... It may be only an apparent piety, the unconscious refuge of a spiritual and intellectual poverty which, once their surroundings have been changed, will show up their unreliability. We would insist that educators keep an especially watchful eye on unreliable natures, in order to discern whether it is merely the inconstancy proper to youthfulness, which is particularly evident in the years of physical growth, or whether it is constitutional, the sort found in certain adolescents who apply themselves to a thousand things without persevering in any of them, exceedingly unstable, always hesitant and undecided, showing all the signs of an underlying nervous instability' (second paragraph).

is a tendency to be shocked and blame young people for thinking too much, asking questions about everything and taking insufficient notice of the experience of their elders. Or incriminations may be made about previous directors or novice-masters for not having made their charges immune from such deviations or extravagances. This is simply an attempt to avoid responsibility. It is utopian to expect the initial formation to remove all difficulties and produce an infallible and irrevocable decision. The years of formation give candidates a chance to realize their talents and gifts and show their capacities, and this means that certain difficulties are inevitable and even necessary if real growth is to be assured. Nothing can be done without personal effort.

In addition, it is enjoined that this 'tutiorism' 'so clearly expressed in so many ecclesiastical documents, both general and particular', should be observed when dealing with cases of doubtful vocations (third paragraph).

Finally, even when the shortage of candidates seems to urge a relaxation of the requirements, this tutiorism is justified by a double consideration: 'While it is true that the Sacraments do not draw their efficacity from the priest's own personal value, it is no less true that the furtherance of Christian life is closely bound up with the holiness of the ministers of God, whose mission, according to the Gospel precept, consists precisely in bringing light and preserving from corruption, not simply by the means provided by grace but also by the example of their own lives (Matt., 5: 13-14) ... Preoccupation with numbers as opposed to quality proves, moreover, to be a wrong calculation. The introduction even of moderately satisfactory priests in the sacred ministry has a depressing effect not only upon the zeal of their colleagues, whose apostolic urge will be held back, but especially upon the religious life of the people, the intensity of which is a necessary condition for the flowering of numerous and choice vocations. It is an undeniable fact that vocations flower where true men of God make the ideal that they preach shine forth in its full, unsullied attractiveness ... It should, then, be perfectly clear that preoccupation with numbers, when it succeeds in compromising quality in any way, sins against itself, by progressively drying up the ground which is most suited for the growth of vocations and by setting up an obstacle to the very action of divine grace.'

Problems of psychological and spiritual growth

But great watchfulness is important when such problems do appear. It may well be that the question raised is serious and lays bare a deeply-rooted deficiency. Steps must then be taken to assess its bearing on the vocation.

Is it true, as some claim, that all this can be left to one side when the problems seem minor, even though they are persistent? And what is to be done when the number of years already spent in the seminary or religious life argue against returning to the world or making any sort of break? We must seek a sound approach to such eventualities.

The problems which crop up should be accepted naturally and without surprise: clashes with their companions, recriminations against authority, unexpected sexual urges, crises about religion or faith. The inevitably 'closed' atmosphere of any house of formation is liable to exasperate the difficulties or make them grow out of all proportion. And anyway, problems which may seem trivial or baffling should never be minimized: no difficulty can be called minor when the candidate in question feels it to be important.

A seminarist may complain that the female figure, which till then has left him indifferent, is now disturbing him. If he is listened to, he will be helped to realize that he has never seen sexuality as a positive value. Starting from a minor problem like this, he sees the necessity of refashioning his way of thinking, which he has hitherto been unaware of. Any attempt to put his mind at rest by telling him not to think about it any more will only make his anxiety worse, or else end in repression, with all the attendant consequences.

A young religious may complain of distraction in prayer, although he found prayer so easy in the noviciate. His director will not relieve him with the magic formula: 'Remain scrupulously faithful to the times appointed for prayer and everything will come right in due course.' On the contrary, he must help him form a clear idea about what his prayer has been. The young religious then discovers that he had been making systematic reflections, more philosophical than religious, about one or other truth of faith. At the time this suited his temperament, but it was establishing no real contact with God. He now realizes that the ease he had claimed in prayer was artificial, and urged on by this discovery he gradually regains possession. At last he has realized what prayer is all about. The director, of course, could have brushed it all aside ('Everyone suffers from distraction; it's simply a question of not giving in to it deliberately') or tried to coax him ('I'm afraid it's like that for all of us; just offer this tiresome little cross to our Lord'). He would have solved the problem the easy way, but the candidate would have gained nothing.

Another candidate may put forward the human motives which helped to make up his initial decision to embrace religious life. He is worried about the purity of his intention and whether he was right to commit himself. But he seems in all respects quite suitable and deeply spiritual. Here again, he should not be sent away with the assurance that in the opinion of those responsible he is certainly doing the right thing. It is surely better to take advantage of the opportunity given to underline the value of a personal attitude which is constantly purifying itself of any considerations of self. It should be made clear that a vocation is grace at work in the soul: any decision taken now with full knowledge will triumph over past failings, even big ones. There is no need to put the past right, even if this could be done. The important thing is that the awareness of an insufficient motivation in the past should lead the candidate to make a well-considered decision with the motives he has at present.

These three examples all end in a positive recognition of spiritual development, and they have been given intentionally. But the possibility is not excluded that sexual integration might have been unattainable, that prayer might have been non-existent and certain to remain so, and that the motivation might by now have lost its appeal. This shows how valuable it is to pay attention to minor difficulties.

Sometimes superiors and directors protest that the candidates have been told all these things time and again in community instructions and personal interviews and yet seem so slow in accepting them—why should they be so keen on finding everything out for themselves when they only needed to have listened? After all, what they ultimately discover is more or less what they have always been taught. As a result, the superiors and directors are quite put out or remain completely stupefied when young people, timidly or proudly as the case may be, admit their discovery and punctuate their triumph by exclaiming: 'Why did no one ever tell us?'

Both sides forget that it is not enough to state the truth—it must be understood as well. But no one understands what is said unless it can awaken some personal echo, and this echo is only possible through personal experience. There must be no illusion about this. Candidates should not be accused of inattentiveness or perversity. It is a cause for rejoicing when they have at last discovered for themselves what their guides themselves had to discover before they could make it the substance of their own spiritual lives.

Difficulties just before final commitment

Emphasis has been laid up till now on the minor problems which may present themselves at any time during the years of formation. But there are also persistent doubts and serious difficulties which only come to light after many years, and sometimes just before the final step is to be taken.

Many directors seem inclined to minimize their importance, attributing them to the strain of preparation or to tiredness after

a long period of studying. So they recommend the candidates to
think about something else; the change of surroundings and
activities which will soon come is presented as a cure-all. Uncertainty disappears, they say, once the decisive step is made; any
preoccupations will vanish in the heat of the apostolate—and so
the candidate should go on without any misgivings and grace will
do the rest.

This sort of reasoning tends to forget that the end of formation
and the imminence of the final commitment can cause the breaking
of a long and serious reticence. Many candidates enter the seminary
without seeing any difference between the boarding-school they
have just left and the one they are now entering. They need to be
faced with the immediate prospect of their final commitment before they come to a rude awakening. Religious, generally speaking,
notice a greater change, although it may happen that the
atmosphere of the minor seminary has led quite naturally to
their entering the noviciate. Others have been carried away by their
enthusiastic impulse and have, as it were, taken the difficulties of
the noviceship in their stride. Admitted as good candidates to their
first vows, they have seen their somewhat overrated effort relaxed,
and their short-lived ardour extinguished, during the years of
study. They have probably told themselves time and again that they
must talk to their director about it but their good resolutions
have never come to anything. Now they wake up with a jolt and
rub their eyes. Some want at all cost to make up for time wasted
as fast as they can, others remain quite stupefied or simply stagger
and collapse.

Whatever the candidates' reaction at the time and whatever may
have led up to it, the real seriousness of their case must not be
minimized. The many years spent in the seminary or religious life
do not present an extenuating circumstance. Far from it. The fact
that the awakening has taken so long indicates that the trouble

goes deep and only comes to the surface under pressure of over-whelming circumstances.

The best recommendation in such cases is generally to call in a specialist—a doctor if psychological factors are at work, or a priest if the crisis is of a religious nature. They will be able to arrive at a more impartial estimate of the causes. Superiors and directors who have been following the candidate's progress for several years are inevitably at a disadvantage through the ties of familiarity that have been formed.

If a candidate is so disturbed that he wants to leave immediately, he should not be kept against his will. The wisest thing, though, is to urge him to act without undue haste and suggest that he puts off his commitment for a year. During this time greater attention can be paid to how he pulls himself together, and he can be helped to decide on what he must do with his mind more at rest. The fact that the years spent in the seminary or religious life have given no cause for complaint cannot be used as an argument for keeping him on. Candidates who immediately put this argument are un-consciously trying to hide their real fear of the responsibilities of life.

In no case is it permissible to put an end to the difficulty by an official *fiat*. If they are led by persuasion or injunction to commit themselves once and for all, the way lies open for the worst possible consequences. Superiors and directors who in such cases sub-stitute themselves for their charges, are doing them irreparable harm—particularly when the subjects have begged them to do so or welcomed their action enthusiastically. The consequences of a person being so fundamentally alienated from what he has taken on will last for the rest of his life. When, however, the candidate shows himself incapable of understanding the seriousness of the im-pediments and of asking to be released, the superiors can and even must send him away. The unwavering firmness which is required is not incompatible with kindness and sympathy.

5. AFTER THE FINAL COMMITMENT

Ideally speaking, final commitments ought to put an end to all hesitation or doubt. But in this life the ideal is never fully realized. On the part of superiors and subjects alike, good faith can be taken unawares. Falsehood, even, can creep in. These are the plain facts. Often, very soon after their ordination or final vows, priests or religious come to ask for advice or suddenly reveal their despair, because they think or are afraid that they have been wrong about their vocation.

It goes without saying that we do not include people who are disconcerted by the inevitable gloomy days (or 'dark nights') with which any growing spiritual life is familiar. It has already been emphasized many times that any genuine vocation is a lifegiving grace to which a man conforms himself as well as he can. It is a sign of life when new problems arise unceasingly and are resolved with increasing clarity. It is hardly surprising if they occur also in priests and religious who are attentive to the motions of grace and open their hearts wide to it. Any new experience of God's action enlightens those who are favoured by it about their past insufficiencies. The more the fullness of God is imparted, the more glaring one's personal failings seem.

These painful experiences of self-renunciation, however, have a distinctive characteristic. A wide-awake director will not have much trouble in discerning it; even the person he is directing realizes it, without being able to put it into words very well. On reflection they both discover that violent emotional upheavals arise because God seems to have removed all contact with him, and this is what so often brings the suffering to its height. Nevertheless there is a certainty in the depths of the being. It cannot be directly reached, but it does nonetheless provide a firm foundation. It sustains and nourishes unshakable faith, imperturbable hope and inexhaustible charity. However painful such a trial may be, it is enriching. The spiritual director must understand it if he is not to deaden it, and the person concerned must accept it if he is to let it bear fruit.

None of these genuinely religious experiences have anything in common with the doubts and uncertainties about vocation which we are about to deal with. They belong to the sphere of spiritual direction in the strict sense. They must be judged and put right according to the rules laid down by eminent spiritual directors out of their own experience. St John of the Cross and St Ignatius Loyola spring at once to mind, but many other names could be suggested.

Possible crises, their origin and their meaning

The crises which will be discussed in the following paragraphs have a completely different origin. They come to a head because it is no longer possible to maintain that the call which had been claimed or believed in is genuine. They can in fact be reduced to three categories. These will first be described, and then we will give some details about the sort of help which can be given.

First of all there are the candidates who have always been more or less hesitant or uncertain, but they have never dared face the problem squarely. They considered that even to question their vocation was a temptation to be instantly repelled. Or they may have been put in a position which has made it impossible for them to speak openly. They have been told often enough that they had nothing to worry about, that the superior and spiritual director would vouch for them, and that everything would sort itself out at the moment they finally commited themselves or left their period of probation behind. They have impatiently counted the days to his ordination or profession which would bring release. To their confusion they have found that the final sacrament or consecration is no more of a healer than time itself. In the end they are in a state of panic about the final step.

Others had settled down comfortably in their period of formation. They have been rudely shaken up from their lethargy by the unsuspected demands, the unavoidable responsibilities and the unforeseeable burdens of the life of a priest or formed religious. They try to block up the gaps as well as they can and make a more or less cosy nest for themselves. There they vegetate without too much trouble simply because they manage to do nothing worthwhile. More often they groan under the task weighing on them, or at their own depressing inadequacies. Some take refuge in neurasthenia, others defend themselves by criticism, scepticism or a latent spirit of rebellion.

Finally there are those who have always been vaguely aware of some diriment impediment. For lack of courage or insight they have been unable to face it, give it a name or put it right during the years of formation. They now feel they have been caught in their own trap. They react to their laxity by looking for scapegoats. They throw the blame on superiors who were not sufficiently shrewd or watchful, or on God 'who let it all happen'.

The help to be given by superiors and directors

Those who have to help these people should receive them with boundless patience. They should not let themselves be nonplussed by their bitter remarks or their frantic grievances. Nor should they be taken in by the nonchalant attitude they assume or the self-sufficiency they affect. Culpability, sometimes very real, should not be stressed at the outset: enough torment is being endured without the need to add any more. Beware of seeming to agree with them too much or to share in their recriminations against directors or superiors. Without contradicting, bring them face to face with the situation as it really is, for nothing is changed by accusations in the air or allegations that cannot be checked.

In cases of the first type, and particularly if the crisis comes to a head fairly soon after the final step, the nature of the problem must be investigated very thoroughly. But prudence is needed. The person concerned should be brought to see the reasons for a thorough and impartial examination and accept, if necessary, the conclusion that the motivation has been obviously insufficient. It will otherwise be impossible to dispel the ambiguity which is at the root of the trouble.

It should be noted, however, that doubts are not being cast on the validity of the ordination or profession. The objective fact is not being put to the test but only the subjective dispositions of the subject. Only in an atmosphere of truth can progress be made by leading him to accept the situation and renew his intention to give himself unreservedly.

This sort of process is made no easier by the fact that the decision is already irrevocable (at any rate as regards the priesthood). A patience which will withstand all tests, a genuine reception of what is revealed without causing discouragement and a supernatural viewpoint free from any false compromise or purely rationalistic approach often succeed in establishing peace of mind which, extending beyond mere resignation to what cannot be repaired, can open the way to a fundamental acceptance of the situation. Such cases can sometimes be brought to a successful conclusion by an experienced priest, provided no undue psychological factors are at work.

Cases of the second and third types are more difficult still to handle, because psychological factors do play a predominant, if not exclusive, part. Their treatment generally requires specialized training. Only trained psychotherapists (priests or laymen) are in a position to obtain a lasting improvement. But no miracles should be expected. Specialists cannot act as substitutes for their clients; they can only help them to find their bearings again and to take their futures in their own hands.

Collaboration between specialists and directors is vitally necessary if there is to be any hope of a real cure—collaboration in which each necessarily respects the other's territory. At the beginning of treatment the priest must keep in the background. All he can do can be summed up in a few words: emphasize the necessity of the treatment, refuse to let himself be led by the subject to contradict the doctor, and give completely objective answers to questions concerning spiritual matters. If the treatment goes favourably the subject will not turn very often to the spiritual director. This is a good sign. If, however, there is difficulty in making a start, the subject will keep on turning to the priest, who must then gently but firmly send him back for the treatment he is trying to escape.

It can be seen that the work of the specialist and the priest complement one another, and needs more than regular contact for talking over the case and deciding the attitude to be taken in face of this particular situation. To take charge of such direction the priest should preferably be both acute and sensitive; he should also be well informed about the nature of psychological treatment so that he will not intrude into it, but will remain in the background while it is going on.

Laïcization

A negative and insubordinate attitude, bitter accusations and unjustified recriminations are frequently associated with crises of vocation which arise after the final commitment. The director and the superior may be tempted to have recourse to laïcizing someone who is a notably thankless task; all the more so if he takes a delight in saying that he will feel released, and enabled—as soon as he can put off the religious or priestly habit as he ingenuously puts it—to behave like 'ordinary people'. This assertion is fallacious, as experience shows.

Laïcization, in itself, brings no solution to the problems. It is, and always will be, the last shift. That much is obvious. The causes which make a person long for it as a liberation or cling to it as a gleam of hope are too deeply rooted in personal attitudes to be put right by a mere change of surroundings. So it should never be advocated for reasons of convenience, such as shaking off subjects who are difficult to handle. Before this step can be sanctioned, the advantages which accrue from it must be seen to counterbalance the disadvantages. The advantages can be said to predominate, for instance, when the fulfilment of the exterior obligations of life in a community or in the priesthood aggravate the subject's difficulties to the point where they become unbearable.

In other cases, however, it is usually preferable to help the unfortunates to discover a personal attitude and find a therapy which will give them some support, or some treatment which will relieve them sufficiently so that they are no longer crushed under the weight of their troubles. But no illusions should be entertained about the results—it will always be a heavy cross for the subject, for those responsible for him and for the whole community.

Of course, if the subject demands to be allowed to go, he cannot be forced to stay. The chances of getting him to stay freely are better if a completely objective examination can be made of the advantages of his possible departure. Certain directors, who put too much stress on the—admittedly very real—difficulties he will encounter in his new situation, will only precipitate departure or even flight. If, however, the person gives way to their urgings, he will be vaguely aware that once again an inauthentic factor has carried him to a decision.

Any help of this nature is extremely complicated. Where it is humanly possible, it is advisable to seek advice from specialists.

These should not be merely psychologists, but men well-informed about religious life, so that they can assess exactly what factors are causing the trouble. Otherwise they will only incriminate religious life as such, which solves nothing and is false into the bargain. And they should not be simply moralists: they must know enough psychology to be able to surmise what psychological causes are at work. Otherwise, they are liable to reduce every problem to the moral plane, which is one further burden for the victims. A psychological failing is not necessarily an infidelity to grace, nor a sin freely consented to.

The complexity of all these painful crises cannot be underestimated. To reduce them to one single factor (pride, vanity, jealousy, unbridling of instincts, a weak will, instability of character, etc.) is an over-simplification. The origin of the trouble often lies ten or twenty years back, if not more. If he is to give appropriate assistance the consultant priest must have at his command an advanced training in both spirituality and psychology which has been tested and completed by practical experience.*

The few details that have been put forward bear only on the discernment of vocations. Certainly it would be a good thing if a pastoral theology could be worked out for 'stray shepherds', but it is not within the scope of this book to develop it. Any desire to touch on the subject in a few lines would be not only rash but harmful, since we could give no idea of the different applications needed in each case.

---

* An admirable enterprise was undertaken a few years ago in France. It was the opening of a medico-psychological centre which sets out to help priests suffering from psychic disturbances, although not actually affected by mental illness. Doctors and priests work together at this centre (established at Cambo in the Basses-Pyrénées), and its purpose and functioning are described in the *Supplément de la Vie Spirituelle,* no. 46, 1958, pp. 355-68.

THE DISCERNMENT OF VOCATIONS AS A WORK OF COLLABORATION

In the last analysis the discernment of vocations is always a verification: In which direction is such and such a man's life intended to go by divine grace? This direction becomes evident on two planes, one external, the other internal. It must be asked whether he has the necessary aptitudes and whether God has seen fit to call him.

Throughout this work we have gone into a great number of facts which must be taken into consideration. At the same time an attempt has been made to discover their proper significance and the general bearing they have on the situation as a whole. The work of analysis must be put together again by a synthesis, or else the elements will be scattered instead of being fused together in a stable, balanced and harmonious way.

But this is not enough. In practice many people with various qualifications contribute to the discerning of a vocation. If their interventions are to lead to a really satisfactory conclusion, it is most important that they should be animated by the same spirit. Any divergence in their views compromises the value of their decisions: this is why the documents all urgently recommend those responsible to co-ordinate their efforts. To this end they must study closely and with one mind the problems which arise, in order to agree on a uniform line of conduct. Collaboration of this sort does not by any means demand lengthy discussions of each individual case—after all, some of those responsible are bound by professional or sacramental secrecy. Real collaboration is a matter of each person complementing the work of others. If all those responsible know and respect each other's respective territories, each can carry out his own task even where there is no possibility of discussing the particular case to be solved. This is most important.

So we will bring this study to an end with a final survey of the whole subject. I will summarize briefly what is expected from the main categories of people who have to do with discerning vocations. Religious and nuns, from whom reports and information are required; the priests approached by candidates before entry; superiors and reverend mothers; spiritual directors; ordinary confessors who are not directors; priests consulted occasionally by people who are in their period of formation; and finally specialists, priests or laymen, who are turned to because of their personal competence in one sphere or another.

Anyone who has consecrated himself to God in a form of life, be it monastic, apostolic or secular, owes it to himself on account of his very state of life, to know the principles which govern the discernment of vocations and understand how they apply to himself. If he does not, he will never be able to assume responsibility and commit himself personally by a freely given response to the impulses of grace. A first-hand knowledge of the life as it is lived and of everything to do with vocation is necessary for him, in the first place on his own personal account. And then this knowledge will allow him to give entirely objective answers to the questions of those who, impressed by his example, feel the urge to model themselves on him or even follow him. Such personal familiarity with the ways of grace and how to recognize them in practice is always presupposed in those people who are mentioned below.

All priests receive a general mandate by the very jurisdiction which is conferred on them. It is their duty to enlighten anyone who comes to them and shows a desire to enter the priesthood or religious life. But they are not to forget that they only play an instrumental rôle. Certainly it falls on them to make various points quite clear: what a vocation is; what the providential meaning of aptitudes is; how to recognize, at least provisionally, whether grace is at work or not in the impulses which are felt. But they must refrain from any interference. It is not for them to decide about a candidate's vocation or to set his mind in any particular direction. They have no right to impose their own preferences or personal inclinations or to bring in considerations which have nothing to do with discerning vocations: the pressing needs of apostolic work, shortage of vocations, the particular needs of various countries, and so on. By following what seems to be the likely course of grace, they should help the candidate to decide for himself and to commit himself to a 'probation' which offers the greatest possibility of success. This does not detract from the part a priest has to play, which is to lead the candidate towards the point where he can reach his own decision with full knowledge of the facts. This personal decision must, of course, remain subordinate to that which will be made by the competent superior with an official mandate from the Church.

The authorities (bishops and major superiors, as well as their collaborators) hold their official mandate either from their function or a duly instituted delegation. They also must know the full extent of this mandate, or they will be in danger of escaping the responsibility imposed on them. It is for them to assess the physical and mental aptitudes and the spiritual stability of the candidates who offer themselves or who are already in their period of formation. They can, of course, turn to doctors, psychologists or priests for specialized opinions; it is very desirable and often indispensable to do so in doubtful cases. But medical or psychological examination does not absolve superiors from their responsibility. They must keep a watchful eye on any matters like these during the years of formation. The Church explicitly says that the discernment of vocations must be exercised until perpetual vows or ordination. It belongs to them, therefore, to judge whether a candidate's state of health is satisfactory, availing themselves of the assistance of qualified doctors where the need is felt. In this decision they will reckon with the particular requirements of their way of life, and with the possible repercussions of so-called 'minor' indispositions. They will likewise have to follow closely the psychological development of those entrusted to their care. If a doubt comes to light, they will use the criteria drawn from a candidate's general behaviour and filled in by the negative symptoms of either family or personal origin to see whether there are reasons for sending him away, or whether it would be preferable to ask for a specialist to examine him. In doubtful cases the Church's requirements are explicit. All doubts must be settled before final admission; if not, dismissal is imperative. Anxious for their subjects' well-being, superiors should not excessively prolong the periods of trial, the only purpose of which is to set doubts at rest. On the other hand, they should not use the fact that the first years of formation have given no reason to suspect any difficulties as a pretext for ignoring problems which arise later. They must never forget that everything to do with external vocation is in their department. External does not mean adventitious: it is an integral part of divine vocation, just as much as internal vocation is.

Spiritual directors must above all be on the watch for the flowering of the life of grace. What they must do is help those who have already been admitted to the seminary or the religious life. Primarily they must further the identification of their charges with the type of life they have chosen; by doing so they can check whether this identification is following a genuine course. Thus they should help their charges to recognize and purify their motivation, and together with them examine whether their spiritual progress attests the authenticity of their initial decision and the presence of grace at work in them. Their function may well bind them to secrecy, and this is a further reason for making their charges face up to their personal responsibility. What has just been said about spiritual directors applies, *mutatis mutandis,* to novice-masters and mistresses and all who are responsible for those who have taken their first vows.

In many cases the ordinary confessors of religious and nuns are not spiritual directors. Their function, then, is primarily sacramental. The Church, however, reminds them that they have a double responsibility. As confessors they must form their judgments at the sacramental level and they can and must absolve any penitent who shows sincere contrition. But as confessors to religious and nuns they must point out to their penitents the faults which can constitute a serious obstacle to the type of life they have embraced. If the penitent, duly warned, does not succeed in putting matters right, the confessor is bound in conscience to remind him of his duty. He must insist that his penitent should go to his director or superior and either submit the problem to them or inform them that he is leaving the house of formation on the advice of his confessor.

There are yet other priests who come into contact with seminarists, religious or nuns during their period of formation on particular occasions: among others, retreat-givers and extraordinary confessors. It is normal for their advice to be asked or for problems to be laid before them, for this, after all, is one of the purposes of their ministry. These priests, therefore, need not be evasive—but they must make allowance for their particular situation. Circumspection is necessary. Where possible they should strive to see the problem with clarity and help the person consulting them to find an adequate solution. Never, though, may they take the place of the superior, director or ordinary confessor. When faced with complicated problems, they must undertake to explain the principles at stake and their implications. They should help a candidate, above all, to see matters sufficiently clearly to be able to submit the difficulty quite openly to his habitual director or to his superior. Their transient help will never be effective if this condition is not fulfilled.

Specialists, called in for consultation, act as advisers. Priests or laymen—theologians, moralists, canon lawyers, doctors, psychologists—they must be aware of the scope of the intervention required of them. They are not asked to pronounce on the vocation as such, but to give as nicely judged an opinion as possible, with the intention of throwing light on whatever the doubtful factor may be. From the outset they must see that the terms of secrecy demanded by the candidate are known, particularly when he is sent by his superiors. On the other hand, superiors must not forget that any consultant specialist is and remains bound by secrecy as long as the patient does not personally release him, of his own free will.

This list of the principal categories of people who contribute towards the discernment of vocations reveals the diversity of their tasks. Sometimes, in particular cases, the Church permits a superior or novice-master to assume functions which are usually given to others. These exceptional provisions cannot be dealt with here: they vary with the religious family in question. But even then, those responsible for discernment are still numerous. This is another reason why they should never lose sight of the fundamental unity and common inspiration of their activity. The moment all those responsible realize that their various tasks complement one another, they will join in pursuit of one and the same goal. For all of them have to recognize, verify and foster the authenticity of the operations of divine grace in the candidate in question. He, in the first place, is the reason for their collaboration. Their sole aim is to help anyone who wants to know the will of God, to see it clearly and to give themselves wholly to it. There must be no mistake: although the discernment of vocations is primarily an ecclesiastical function, it can only be carried out fully if the person who is its object identifies himself fully with the will of God. It is for him, freely and without evasion, to assume his responsibility before the Lord. Fot it is in him that grace is at work; it is also in him and with him that the action of God has to be verified. With the guidance of the Church and its authorized representatives he must discern the impulse of grace in order to yield to it without any reserve. He will discover, as the case may be, that God is leading him towards the life of religious consecration, the life of a priest, or the life of a Christian in the world.

And it is for this reason that any prudent and valid discernment of vocation ends with a positive decision. It makes possible an authentic self-commitment to the direction given by grace to each individual life. The forms of life are certainly many and varied. But all life proceeds from the Father, to whom, under the impulse of the Holy Spirit whom he sends us, we are led back again by the one and only Saviour, our Lord Jesus Christ.

RETREAT-GIVING

A PRIEST'S part in the discernment of vocations varies with the responsibilities laid upon him. He may be a superior, a director or an adviser. But it should not be forgotten that these responsibilities themselves imply other functions. To pass these by in silence would be to risk distorting the spiritual outlook which this book has tried to respect in all points. It may seem at first sight that some of these functions do not allow a full application of the principles analysed up to now.

The superior, the spiritual director and even the adviser are called upon, more or less regularly, to give religious instructions or spiritual conferences to the communities or groups entrusted to their care. What procedure is to be followed to avoid any collision with the principles of discerning vocations, without at the same time detracting from the specific character of exhortations and retreats?

To avoid ambiguity, we must draw a distinction between these two things, without, however, declaring them to be irreconcilable. By being different, they complement one another.

It is evident that the retreat-giver who addresses young men or women both can and must show how magnificent a generous response to the call of God is. He is perfectly justified in presuming that some of his hearers have been especially cultivated by grace. His words may let these ones see that their hidden aspirations are of a specifically religious nature. God uses his words to make them personally aware of a call which had passed unnoticed or been inadequately interpreted. With even more reason, then, superiors and spiritual directors should perform a similar task in their exhortations to the community. They do not need to draw attention to the call so much as to further a total and unconditional commitment.

Everyone, however—the retreat-giver as well as the superior and the director—should take care to be moderate. Any exhortation seeks to win over, but by so doing runs the risk of giving way to oratorical flourishes, heavily weighted arguments, cutting remarks and exaggerated descriptions, all of which is to the detriment of exact information and honest persuasion. It inevitably distorts the minds and hearts of uncritical hearers and at the same time puts off those who are more knowing. But even where no extravagant words spoil the exhortation, the task of the retreat-giver is and remains specific. He must state the truth clearly, attractively and in a way suitably adapted to his audience. He should encourage his hearers to put it into practice and live according to its spirit. The discernment of vocations involves something more than mere information, however invigorating this may be. It sets out, together with the subject who is familiar with its basic principles, to discover how to discern the attractions of grace which must guide him in applying these principles to his own case.

In fact, if the functions of retreat-giving and discerning vocations were never united in the same person, the danger arising from their confusion would be considerably reduced.

But the retreat-giver who has spoken with fire and enthusiasm will, it is to be hoped, receive those of his hearers who think or feel sure that they have detected in his words of echo of God's call. From then on his function changes. It is not that he has to rebuff or discourage those he has kindled. But now that his warm encouragements have borne fruit, he must gradually progress towards an interior discernment—his exhortations will give way to a sounding of the motions of internal grace. If he does not have the time to do this himself, it is sufficient for him to show vocation in its true light as a freely given answer to a call coming from God. It will then be for the spiritual director, the adviser or the superior who is supervising the admission to verify the probable authenticity of the call.

The superior—and the same applies to the spiritual director— who has just shown in very clear relief the demands of generosity and fidelity, must then welcome his new charges. If he maintains the same tone in private conversation, it may happen that his powerful personality or his infectious enthusiasm overwhelms the person he is talking to, and roots him to the spot instead of promoting a freely undertaken self-commitment.

Whatever the task he has to perform, a priest has two functions: that of arousing vocations and that of discerning them. It is only right that he should know how they differ. There is nothing surprising about this distinction: it has been realized by spiritual writers of all ages.

We quote only one testimony, that of St Ignatius, who had in this matter an experience quite out of the ordinary.★ In the *Spiritual Exercises* the discernment of vocations occupies a central position. These were and still are made with the intention of finding the will of God by putting the exercitant's life in order. They culminate in the choice of a state of life.

At the very beginning of the *Exercises*, St Ignatius warns the priest who watches over the exercitant to be on his guard against any interference when the creature is talking with his Creator. And he urges this attitude for the task of those whose business is

---

★ Only one text is being given to illustrate this distinction. It should be noted, however, that St Ignatius's attitude is to be found also in St John of the Cross, as has been very well demonstrated by Father Lucien-Marie de Saint-Joseph in a contribution to *Etudes Carmélitaines. Direction spirituelle et psychologie*, Paris, 1951, pp. 173-205.

not, in the first instance, to interpret the personal call which is making itself heard in the soul.

He gives these details about the two functions we have just distinguished: 'The giver of the Exercises ought not to move the receiver rather to poverty or promise of any such thing than to the opposites, nor to one state or mode of living rather than to another; because, though apart from the Exercises we may lawfully and meritoriously urge all, who are probably fitted for it, to choose continence, virginity, religious life, and all manner of perfection; nevertheless in such Spiritual Exercises it is more suitable and much better in seeking the divine will, that the Creator and Lord Himself should impart Himself to His devout soul, embracing her to His love and praise, and disposing her for the way in which she can better hereafter serve Him. Thus the giver of the Exercises should not lean nor incline himself either to one side or the other, but keeping steady midway, like a beam of a balance, should allow the Creator to work directly with the creature and the creature with her Creator and Lord.'★

There is, then, no contradiction between the function of the priest who gives a retreat, whatever office he is called on to fill at other times, and that of the priest who has to ascertain the presence of a vocation. Although preaching and retreat-giving are necessary for the spreading of truth, it is just as necessary that grace should act in the soul if this truth is to be grasped. A priest is officially appointed to teach others the fact that grace works and also to

---

★*The Spiritual Exercises of St Ignatius Loyola*,' Fr. Joseph Rickaby, S.J., London, Burns and Oates, Ltd., 1915.

When this text is being read, it should be remembered that the 'director' is not a retreat-giver addressing a more or less homogeneous group of hearers, but a spiritual director who watches a single person over many days given over to recollection and prayer, with the aim of finding the will of God by the ordering of his life. Retreats—or spiritual exercises made in a group—are a variation, approved by the Church, of the Exercises which, originally, were made individually.

describe its operations. But he, too, must learn, in all submission, the ways in which it operates, by allowing the person who consults him to find out for himself the direction in which grace is leading him in his own individual case.

THE French text of this book was already set when the Congregation of the Holy Office published a *Monitum* dated 15th July, 1961. The fourth paragraph concerns matters which are dealt with here. As the text in question is an official one whose exact implications have unfortunately been distorted by the press, the original words will now be reproduced as they appeared in the *Osservatore Romano* of 16th July. A close translation follows:

'Improbanda est opinio eorum qui autumant praeviam institutionem psychoanalyticam omnino necessariam esse ad recipiendos Ordines Sacros, vel proprie dicta psychoanalytica examina et investigationes subeunda esse candidatis Sacerdotii et Professionis Religiosae. Quod valet etiam si agatur de exploranda aptitudine requisita ad sacerdotium vel religiosam professionem. Similiter sacerdotes et utriusque sexus Religiosi psychoanalystas ne adeant nisi Ordinario suo gravi de causa permittente.'

'It is necessary to condemn the opinion of those who claim that a previous psychoanalytical formation is indispensable for the reception of holy orders, or that examinations and investigations of a strictly psychoanalytical nature must be undergone by candidates for the priesthood or religious life. The same reservation applies when these examinations are made with a view to recognizing aptitude for the priesthood or religious profession. Likewise, priests, religious and nuns may not turn to a psychoanalyst unless their Ordinary permits it for a serious reason.'

These words of the Holy Office are to put people on their guard against any infatuation with psychoanalysis, and this is only reasonable. Excessive enthusiasm can be just as disastrous as irrational aversion. Psychoanalytical treatment is something too serious to be undertaken lightly and without sufficient motive. The rule issued by the Holy Office corresponds to what has generally been the practice, but it has the advantage of being more specific about the precautions which must be taken when such treatment is indicated or necessary.

The demand for psychoanalytical information as a previous condition for admission to the priesthood or religious profession is quite senseless (with apologies for using stronger language than the *Monitum* itself). The examination of doubtful cases—and *a fortiori* of any candidate to the priesthood or religious profession —can be, and usually is, made quite adequately with the aid of psychological methods and a psychiatric anamnesis which have nothing to do with a psychoanalytical examination in the strict sense. This will be realized on re-reading the programme of method described in the note on page 54ff.

It should be observed, however, that the *Monitum* does not forbid psychoanalytical formation or psychoanalytical investigation in the strict sense. It objects, quite rightly, to the unjustified claim that they should be set up as indispensable conditions.